Theories of Discourse

THEORIES OF DISCOURSE

An Introduction

Diane Macdonell

Basil Blackwell

© Diane Macdonell 1986

First published 1986
Reprinted 1987

Basil Blackwell Ltd
108 Cowley Road, Oxford OX4 1JF, UK

Basil Blackwell Inc.
432 Park Avenue South, Suite 1503,
New York, NY 10016, USA

British Library Cataloguing in Publication Data

Macdonell, Diane
    Theories of discourse: an introduction.
    1. Discourse analysis
    I. Title
    415   P302

    ISBN 0–631–14838–8
    ISBN 0–631–14839–6 Pbk

Library of Congress Cataloging in Publication Data

Macdonell, Diane.
    Theories of discourse.

    Bibliography: p.
    Includes index.
    1. Discourse analysis.   2. Knowledge, Theory of.
    I. Title.
    P302.M294   1986   401.41   85–18679
    ISBN 0–631–14838–8
    ISBN 0–631–14839–6 (pbk.)

Typeset by Oxford Publishing Services

Printed in Great Britain by Billing & Sons Ltd, Worcester

Contents

Acknowledgements

I would like to acknowledge the help of those who have commented on drafts of this book. Special thanks are due to Catherine Belsey for her encouragement and assistance, to Lynette Hunter for advice and discussions, and to Norman King for his painstaking criticisms of successive versions. In addition, Terence Hawkes and Patrick Lyons made helpful comments on the manuscript. To students at Glasgow University, who have readily engaged with the issues raised by current theories, thanks are also due. Finally, I am grateful to Claire Andrews and Philip Carpenter for their careful editing and support.

Introduction

In the late 1960s and the 1970s, initially in France, certain shifts took place in the ways of considering how meanings are constructed. The resulting work on discourses and the questions posed by that work have radical implications not only for the disciplines of the humanities, literary studies and the human sciences, but for all knowledge.

What is 'discourse'?

Dialogue is the primary condition of discourse: all speech and writing is social. Within and across countries, discourses differ. As Vološinov, a Russian linguist, wrote in 1930, 'village sewing circles, urban carouses, workers' lunchtime chats, etc., will all have their own type. Each situation, fixed and sustained by social custom, commands a particular kind of organization of audience' (trans. 1973, p. 97). Discourses differ with the kinds of institutions and social practices in which they take shape, and with the positions of those who speak and those whom they address. The field of discourse is not homogeneous.

Discourse is social. The statement made, the words used and the meanings of the words used, depends on where and against what the statement is made: 'in the alternating lines of a dialogue, the same word may figure in two mutually clashing contexts. . . . Actually, any real utterance, in one way or another or to one degree or another, makes a statement of agreement with or a negation of something' (trans. 1973, p. 80). The kind of speech proper to the shop-floor of a factory conflicts with that of the boardroom. Different social classes use the same words in different senses and disagree in their interpretation of events and situations.

Recent work on discourse has gone beyond this, and, while exploring the ways in which discourses are set up historically and socially, it has brought into view other differences in discourse besides those of class. This work has turned its gaze upon what was hitherto considered mainly as a 'neutral' area: the discourses of knowledge.

It is not only that the speech used on the shop-floor conflicts with that in the boardroom. The speech of a hospital patient concerning his or her body differs from that of the doctor. In any institution, there is a distribution and a hierarchy of discourses. Where a pregnant woman wants her childbirth to be natural, her statements and the concepts in which she thinks may conflict with those of the doctor. The field of discourse within an institution is not uniform; and not all the statements made about the woman's pregnancy may be accepted as 'knowledge': the woman may find that her words carry little weight.

In investigating discourses, such as those which exist in and around medical institutions and practices, work undertaken since the sixties has not tried to collect and combine all the statements that are made there: there is no simple unity. A key issue, in several respects, has become that of accounting for 'the positions and viewpoints' from which people speak and 'the institutions which prompt people to speak . . . and which store and distribute the things that are said' (Foucault 1976, trans. 1979, p. 11). In accounting for various discourses, recent work has begun to write the history of those forces which shape our thinking and our knowledge.

A 'discourse', as a particular area of language use, may be

identified by the institutions to which it relates and by the position from which it comes and which it marks out for the speaker. That position does not exist by itself, however. Indeed, it may be understood as a standpoint taken up by the discourse through its relation to another, ultimately an opposing, discourse. Managerial discourse spoken to workers can act against them; spoken to managers, it may still in the end act against workers: and, in such ways, a discourse takes effect indirectly or directly through its relation to, its address to, another discourse.

Moreover, any discourse concerns itself with certain objects and puts forward certain concepts at the expense of others. In delimiting an area of study, the discourse used in literature departments has marginalized popular literature and women's writings. Lecturers and students in such departments who, for reasons of class or gender or for other reasons, find themselves removed from literary critical discourses are now questioning both the object of their studies and the prevailing concept of 'literature'. In so doing they are developing an alternative discourse and knowledge: 'discourse . . . moves, in its historical impetus, by *clashes*' (Barthes 1971, coll. 1977, p. 200). Different discourses elaborate different concepts and categories. Sometimes concepts elaborated within one discourse may be taken up and rethought within another, but often this is not the case (see Hindess and Hirst 1977a, p. 14). The concept of the 'author' as a free creative source of the meaning of a book belongs to the legal and educational forms of the liberal humanist discourse that emerged in the late eighteenth and early nineteenth centuries; it is not a concept that exists within discourses that have developed recently.

But meanings are not only inscribed in processes of speech and writing. While some work has confined itself specifically to these, other work has reflected more generally on 'the sequence, order and interchange of signs', signs which may be verbal or non-verbal (Adlam et al. 1977, p. 46). Whatever signifies or has meaning can be considered part of discourse. Meanings are 'embodied in technical processes, in institutions, in patterns for general behavior, in forms for transmission and diffusion, and in pedagogical forms' (Foucault 1971a, coll. 1977a, p. 200). For example, the distinction prevalent in the humanities between original creativity, on the one hand, and critical and historical writings, on the other, is often embodied in the organization of course structures, reading lists and examination papers. In the library, original literature is usually arranged alphabetically under the author's name, with the appropriate criticism alongside, while more general works are shelved separately by topic. Thus the mind of the author unifying texts valued as creative can easily be found in the library; the topic and, indeed, the class position of less creative writings may be harder to locate. Not just the organization of a library, but any institutional practice and any technique 'in and through which social production of meaning takes place' may be considered part of discourse (Laclau 1980, p. 87). It is probably the case that no real advance is made by extending the conception of discourse too far beyond processes of speech and writing. However, while it may be unhelpful to take as discourse all the non-verbal as well as the verbal construction of meanings occurring in the wider sphere of 'ideological' practices, clearly the two are interconnected and this book will attend to both.

Discourse and literary studies

This book aims to provide methods, concepts and an orientation to encourage the investigation of all discourses, not only those used in education.

For students and lecturers, the discourses which pertain to higher education, and to the disciplines and domains of knowledge current there, have a particular relevance which has been noticeably emphasized by the 'crisis' running through the humanities and human sciences. This crisis, now of some duration, affects disciplines as diverse as psychology, biology, the history of ideas and the study of literature. The situation is worsened where reductions in government spending slow down new developments and prevent a transformation of these fields of study.

Perhaps more than in the other humanities, the crisis in literary studies is being analysed and confronted; so that once more it is fitting to refer to that discipline as an example. Difficulties in this field have in part taken the form of an unease over how to define literature. Humanist discourse, which remains dominant in arts departments, has provided both the problem of 'what is literature?' and an answer to it. In this discourse, 'it is common to see "literature" defined as "full, central, immediate human experience", usually with an associated reference to "minute particulars"' (Williams 1977, p. 45). The definition is humanist in that it assumes that something recognizable as human experience or human nature exists, aside from any form of words and from any form of society, and that this experience is put into words by an author.

Yet there is some inconsistency between this definition and the prevailing modes of categorizing literature, the dominant sense of what texts should be taught. For in the discipline, 'literature' has been marked out by the double distinction, already mentioned, which separates a body of texts from others viewed as factual, and divides high from popular culture. The latter is excluded from literature, and also omitted, at least until recently, have been the majority of texts written by women. Where 'literature' is then defined as 'immediate human experience', we may wonder what 'human' means.

Work on discourse – the work that this book examines and introduces – cannot be made to repair such inconsistencies. Nor can it be called upon to adjudicate between the differing conceptions which, as a result of structuralist and post-structuralist challenges to the humanist definition, are now found in many departments. Structuralism has considered literature as made up of nothing more or less than a set of arbitrary conventions and structures which we learn to read as literary. Post-structuralism suggests literature is the privileged place of subversion of such arbitrary conventions, their dispersion by unconscious desires. Both conceptions negate the possibility that literature can either express or reflect 'immediate human experience'. Even so, these challenges can be absorbed by departments without any fundamental questioning of the priorities and limits of the discipline.

Rather than serving as a general theory to provide a perfect definition in their place, work on discourse offers an orientation which, if acknowledged in such departments, would not take it for granted that something called 'literature' exists naturally and is part of the order of things. The methods and concepts of recent study of discourse make possible an analysis of the discourses, in their relation to institutional practices, through which a division of texts has been marked out and 'literature' has been constituted as the object of a certain enshrinement. Indeed, work on discourse has encouraged the self-criticism now being developed in literary studies: the investigation of the historical ways in which 'literature' has been constructed.[1] More than that, recent theory of discourse is able to suggest why it is that challenges in the humanities, challenges of the kind made, for example, by structuralism, are readily absorbed and do not transform the disciplines – thus the crisis is prolonged and not resolved. If the study of discourse is to assist in overcoming the difficulties which entrap the humanities, it must explore the role of discourse throughout society, rather than focus simply on education.

The aim of this book is to introduce the recent developments which are making possible exactly that wider study of the different and, indeed, contradictory discourses used in society. Such work attends to the effects different discourses have, the political relations in which they take shape, and the positions held by those who use them; it also explores discourses in their connections with various institutions. In introducing such work, this book takes up a point of view which is historical as well as theoretical, and avoids those general notions which would have us believe that the only possible starting-point is discourse itself – for the key advances in the theory of discourse have been neither speculative nor general. Recent theories of discourse are not, however, homogeneous, and some lines of work will be treated critically.

Work on discourse has been careful, even scholarly: precise in drawing lines of argument and detailed in its investigations. But neither precise argument nor thorough research can claim to offer a neutral or natural truth. Indeed, such work finds part of its function in its ability to unmask discourses and knowledges which, from various institutions, and in the face of all the inequality that divides our society (the basic inequality of class, the imposed inequalities of race, gender and religion), claim to speak on behalf of everyone, saying in effect: 'we are all the same: we all speak the same language and share the same knowledge, and have always done so.'

1

The end of the 1960s

Work on discourses indicates that, within a 'language' (for example, within English or French) the words used and the meanings of the words used alter from one discourse to another:

> there is no language in itself, nor any universality of language, but a concourse of dialects, patois, slangs, special languages. There exists no ideal 'competent' speaker-hearer of language, any more than there exists a homogeneous linguistic community. . . . There is no mother tongue, but a seizure of power by a dominant tongue within a political multiplicity. (Deleuze and Guattari 1976, trans. 1981, p. 53)

In its attention to conflicting discourses (varied though this has been), work on discourse has departed from structuralism, as structuralism in its time departed from humanism.

Structuralism's demise

The seminal work of structural linguistics was Saussure's *Course in General Linguistics* (1916, trans. 1974); this was taken up by structuralism in the 1960s. Saussurean linguistics, and some structuralists thereafter, held that a language, such as French, was homogeneous; that, within it, all spoke the same language; and that a common code, or general system of sounds and meanings, underlay the mass of spoken and written utterances. Work on discourse since this time has not rejected all idea of system, but it has rejected the belief that a single and general system lies behind all discourses.

A system is made up of relations. Saussure argued that the sounds, or written images, and the meanings of a language exist only in their relations to each other. They belong to a system of relations, and neither the sounds nor the meanings of words exist before this system; they come from it. To show that meanings do not exist prior to the system of a particular language, Saussure turned to the variety of languages: 'If words stood for pre-existing concepts, they would all have exact equivalents in meaning from one language to the next; but this is not true' (1916, trans. 1974, p. 116). For example, the meaning of the French word *mouton* is not equivalent to that of the English word *sheep*; for English has two words (*sheep* and *mutton*) where French has only one (pp. 115–16). In some languages 'it is not possible to say "sit in the *sun*"' (p. 116).

In arguing that meanings issue from a language, and do not pre-exist it, Saussurean linguistics was a radical departure from earlier theories of meaning. In the eighteenth and nineteenth centuries there were two main kinds of theories of meaning both of which assumed that words stood for pre-existing ideas. One of these asserted that meanings came from things which were 'represented' in words; the other that meanings derived from universal ideas which were 'expressed' in words and given individual form by each speaker. Liberal humanist criticism, in literary studies and throughout the humanities, continues to assume elements from both theories. By demonstrating that meanings vary from one language to another, Saussurean linguistics denied both.

Saussure's linguistics suggested that, within any language, possibilities for meaning are not determined by anything positive (1916, trans. 1974, p. 120). They are marked out only by their negative relations to each other, as if 'yellow' is 'not red', 'not orange', 'not green', and so on: one could go on and on through all the negative possibilities without ever being able to give a positive and definite meaning to 'yellow'. In a system, possibilities for meaning are marked out, but no actual or definite meanings are pinned down.

Many statements in Saussure's *Course* describe language as a system of negative relations, without positive terms. But if all possibilities were free-floating and open, communication could not take place. In resolving this problem, Saussure's *Course* becomes manifestly contradictory, and asserts after all that there are 'positive terms' in language (pp. 120–21). The *Course* considers signs themselves as positive terms, holding that each sound is tied to a meaning in the signs of a language. In the signs, the open possibilities are pinned down, and defined through oppositions (such as presence/absence, black/white, good/bad, etc.) with other signs (p. 121). In this way, the *Course* replaces the initial concept of an open system with that of a closed structure of oppositions. Much of subsequent structural linguistics and structuralism has adopted this view of language.

Structuralism in the sixties was concerned with structures rather than with systems. In the study of narratives, myths or other cultural objects, it looked for a structure of oppositions or positive terms that would be common to all narratives or common to all myths. (For a full consideration of structuralism see Hawkes 1977.)

Structural linguistics did not consider the structure of a language to be evident in reality as something which any one speaker might possess. Absent in itself, the structure was, none the less, present in the utterances it enabled. Structuralism in the study of narrative likewise looked for a general structure that, while absent as such from any one narrative, would enable all narratives. This project implied that the story and characters of a narrative derive from a general structure and do not 'express' ideas in the mind of an author or 'reflect' experience.

Both structural linguistics and structuralism, in varying degrees, therefore refused the dominant humanist conceptions of the author who creates a story to express or reflect 'immediate human experience'. Yet neither fully broke with or proved effective against humanism. Indeed, much of structuralism, despite its sometimes ' "anti-humanist" ideology' had the effect of 'reinforcing the implicit claims of the human sciences to constitute something like the self-evident rationality of the age' (Gordon 1979, p. 24). This happened in several ways. In defining its object of study, the social or communal system of language, Saussure's linguistics used a humanist notion of society, and supposed that anything social was homogeneous and held in common by everyone. Ignoring all conflicts linked (however indirectly) to the class struggle, it was led to ignore even the differences and conflicts between discourses. Indeed, this linguistics, and especially structuralism in seeking a common structure for narratives or myths that would be valid for all time, evacuated history and change, and thereby offered little challenge to the humanist notion of a timeless human nature.

In the movements at the end of the sixties that brought into view the concept of discourse and the conflicts between discourses, there has been a departure from structuralism, but no retreat into humanism. There is no attempt to reinsert the human mind, or the individual author, or things themselves as the source of the meanings of discourses. Discourse is considered as a kind of whole whose organization, at any given stage in history, 'is irreducible either to the history of the careers, thought and intentions of individual agents (the authors of utterances) or to a supra-individual teleology of discovery and intellectual evolution (the truth of utterances)' (Gordon 1979, p. 34). Moreover, discourse is approached in terms of the struggles traversing it, so that the contradictory modes in which it exists as a whole can be studied.

In taking up the historical conditions of meanings, work on discourse has questioned the idea of an abstract and general system or structure of language. Indeed, to posit an overall system or structure of language is to make the conflicts of discourses, in their relation to class and other struggles, inconceivable. A crucial argument concerning discourse is that meanings are to be found only in the concrete forms of differing social and institutional practices: there can be no meaning in 'language'.

Although questioning the idea of a *general* system, the study of discourse does retain a concept of system. Possibilities for meaning are considered to be marked out through a 'system of relationships of substitution, paraphrases, synonymies, etc., which operate between linguistic elements – "signifiers" – in a given discursive formation' (Pêcheux 1975, trans. 1982, p. 112). Different discourses form different systems. Possibilities for meaning are pinned down and made into definite meanings through the social and institutional position from which the discourse comes (and not through a structure of positive terms): 'words, expressions, propositions, etc., change their meaning according to the positions held by those who use them' (p. 111).

Work on discourse both goes beyond and departs from structuralism. Equally, it goes beyond and departs from many of the views of ideology proposed in classic writings of Marxism. How it does so will be examined in later chapters, along with the arguments and procedures of work on discourse. Before this, however, it is appropriate to consider the conditions in France at the end of the sixties and in Britain in the seventies in which such work began to take shape and become, in certain quarters, acceptable.

May 1968 and questions of practice

In France, there was unrest among students in March 1968, as well as in preceding years. But in May of that year the university and education became a major site of struggle. The events of May began with a critique of the university and with student agitation at Nanterre, on the outskirts of Paris, and at the Sorbonne. Lectures and examinations were boycotted, and alternative meetings held. When the disturbances were followed by a workers' strike, quickly mobilizing some ten million, the rebellion in the university gave way to an assault on the whole mode of social organization in France. Factory workers occupied their factories, or came out on strike; the professions followed. There were massive demonstrations, where students' and lecturers' unions joined forces with factory workers, leading to nights of street violence. For a time it looked as if not only the Gaullist regime, but the whole system of State power in France must collapse. Yet, after calling elections, the Gaullists were returned to power at the end of June with an increased majority. The would-be revolution had failed.[1] But the events of May had effects, and work on discourse is one of them.

In retrospect, it is easy to see that investigations of discourse were being made before 1968. Foucault's work since the early sixties had been examining the so-called 'human sciences', their history and their consequences. That work can be read as challenging the 'truth' of the human sciences, by posing questions about the historical conditions in which their discourses emerged. Yet in the early sixties these questions were largely unaccepted. In the university, even those intellectuals who thought of themselves as Marxist tended to take much of their frame of reference, the discipline itself and its objects of knowledge, from the university establishment. The status of the university and its disciplines was largely unexamined. Althusser's 1970 essay on 'Ideology and Ideological State Apparatuses' (coll. 1971) brought about a radical breakthrough in Marxist theory of ideology after 1968. In focusing attention on the institutions of ideology, it located 'the educational apparatus' (the school and the university) as 'the dominant ideological State apparatus in capitalist social formations' (p. 146). And it pointed out how the very content of education could not be neutral.

In the events of May themselves, the critique of the university came mainly from leftist and anarchist positions outside the French Communist Party. It took the form of actions, boycotts and slogans; it was never a fully theorized critique. The students' slogans emphasized spontaneity, imagination and desire. They challenged the aims and methods of the human sciences, psychology and sociology, the prevalence of American concepts. The aims and objectives of modern science were also contested.

The incidents and slogans of May called into question the truth of knowledges. They also raised as an issue the effects of power linked to knowledge – and did so not, or not simply, in terms of university hierarchies, bureaucratic structures and undemocratic institutions. Within the universities, May 1968 was a revolt against everything that acts to tie students to their own specialized knowledges. It was a revolt against university structures, against the content of education, against the disciplines that separate and secure the objects of knowledge – against all that produces a privileged minority of narrow specialists, both isolated from each other and divided from the broad mass of working people.

The student revolt left as a legacy the need to do more than 'dismantle' the university. It turned attention to 'the full range of hidden mechanisms through which a society conveys its knowledge and ensures its survival under the mask of knowledge: newspapers, television, technical schools, and the lycée (even more than the university)' (Foucault 1971b, coll. 1977a, p. 225). Within the university and for intellectuals, the events of May posed the questions of the relation between power and knowledge, and of how education is organized to help keep capitalist society in place. The investigations which were subsequently undertaken went beyond the university, the school or the media.

Since 1968, the questioning of the relation between power and the discourses of knowledge has taken several forms, following along no single line. Indeed, the forces that came together in 1968 and the positions taken up at that time were various. With the events of May beginning in the university, the students constituted a crucial, if in some ways ambiguous, force in the crisis. The strike that ensued was the 'greatest workers' strike in world history' (Althusser 1973, coll. 1976b, p. 35). But the various forces, students, workers and professionals, never quite connected. The student revolt was aimed initially against the institutional practices which make individuals subject to social norms. By and large, the mode of student action was, however, a kind of symmetrical inversion of what it challenged: it was spontaneous, subjective and anarchic. The failure of spontaneity became evident when, after its first wave of enthusiasm was over, the student force quickly fragmented: 'the students found that the spontaneous solidarity created in the streets of Paris was an extremely ephemeral phenomenon' (Johnson 1972, p. 172).

In a sense, the French Communist Party (the PCF) also failed the events of May. Whereas in the particular historical circumstances of the United States and Britain there has been a lack of fusion of Marxist theory with the labour movement and hence no strong Communist party, in France and Europe the Communist party is much more a front-line organization of the working class, with a considerable membership. Yet, confronted with massive strikes, and with demonstrations by workers, students and professionals, the PCF took the view that there was not a revolutionary situation. Moreover, it insisted that workers' demands be limited to wage increases and shorter working hours. This missed the mood of the workers, ignoring their more radical demands. If there can be no revolutionary change without a vanguard party ('one step ahead of the masses, and one step only' – Lenin), none can be effected with a party that lags behind and in its decisions underestimates the masses. In its authoritarian structures and concepts, the PCF was distant from the workers, whose party it was supposed to be. The PCF was a party led from above, deciding policy for the workers and, while deaf to their speech, speaking for them.

Before 1968, in France, it seemed that the role of the progressive intellectual was a similar one: to speak 'the truth to those who had yet to see it, in the name of those who were forbidden to speak the truth: he was conscience, consciousness, and eloquence' (Foucault 1972, coll. 1977a, p. 207). Since 1968, work on discourse in its concepts and its practice has developed in various ways outside this idea of the intellectual who speaks for others. It was through the events of May that a divide between the PCF and a new left, anarchist or reformist, was constructed. As a result, one line of work has largely defined itself by reversing as far as possible the positions taken by the PCF at that time, putting forward the argument that 'only those directly concerned can speak in a practical way on their own behalf' (Deleuze 1972, trans. 1977, p. 209).

Such work on discourse has developed to loosen constraints and to weaken the existing links between power and knowledge, so that other discourses, other knowledges, are not invalidated in advance. Sometimes this has taken the form of theorized critiques of concepts – particularly of the concepts of 'truth' and 'knowledge' – that are used to secure the prestige of certain discourses. Sometimes it has taken other forms. At the beginning of the seventies there were prison revolts in France, as in other countries. In 1971, the Groupe d'Information sur les Prisons (the GIP) was set up, on the initiative of Foucault and other intellectuals who 'became aware of the necessity for confined individuals to speak for themselves' (Deleuze 1972, trans. 1977, p. 206).

In 1975, Foucault's *Discipline and Punish* was published. The book is neither a report of the 'findings' of the GIP nor a history of the prison disturbances. It is a wider study, examining the spread of disciplinary mechanisms since the seventeenth century: the discursive as well as non-discursive techniques through which modern societies train and regulate individuals. It is a comparison of prison, school and factory. As such, it is in some respects a 'relay', an instrument to add strength to the various struggles since May 1968 and to supply arguments and concepts for use elsewhere. Equally, it provides a historical and 'empirical' knowledge of the prison and the school which is far removed from the prevailing knowledge of these institutions, their discourses and practices.

Likewise Castel's *L'Ordre psychiatrique* (1976), an investigation of psychiatric practice and discourse, linked to the resistance to psychiatric institutions and to the Groupe Information Asiles (which, like the GIP, was set up in 1971 to create conditions so that those interned by psychiatry could be heard), provides another knowledge of psychiatry (see Miller 1980). These studies, by developing an alternative knowledge, challenge the prevailing discourses, resisting the way these have solidified into truth.

In the sixties, structuralism attempted, in various ways, to put together a general theory of narrative or a general theory of myth. In so doing, it presupposed that the truth of a theory is guaranteed by an inner logic and that, applied to a given object, theory will yield a knowledge that can be neutral and true. These presuppositions, for all that they are idealist, had also found a way into the PCF, where political practice was taken to be the application of theory. (Problems with these concepts of theory and practice will be examined in chapter 4.)

The questioning of knowledge, which emerged in and through the events of May, called into doubt the ability of a general theory to give knowledge of existing events or objects. Work on discourse has taken shape within, and formulated concepts of, different relations between theory and practice from those available in the sixties. Again, to a large extent, it has been through the questioning of the part played by the PCF in and after 1968 that these different relations between theory and practice have been developed.

In 1972, following the work of the GIP, Deleuze said, 'we're in the process of experiencing a new relationship between theory and practice': practice is no longer to be conceived as 'an application of theory' (trans. 1977, p. 205). The GIP began with certain theoretical propositions. This theoretical discourse was not thereafter applied to prisoners, nor used to decide policies for them. What was practical in the operation of the GIP was the creation of a space in which prisoners could formulate their critique of the prison and be heard. In this, practice became the work of sapping the power of the dominant discourse on prisons, making it possible for the discourse of the prisoners to be effective: 'it is not to "awaken consciousness" that we [intellectuals] struggle . . . but to sap power, to take power'; such activity, it was hoped, could connect ultimately with the struggles of working people, as 'an activity conducted alongside those who struggle for power, and not their illumination from a safe distance' (Foucault 1972, coll. 1977a, p. 208). In the work of the GIP, the relation between theory and practice became interactive and open-ended.

Since the sixties, some of the work on discourse has conceptualized theory as a kind of tool-kit. Theories 'are not a substitute for concrete analysis. They are the tools that make it possible' (Hindess and Hirst 1975, p. 9). Again, since this time, another concept of practice has been developed. While in Marxism political practice is concerned ultimately with changing the social whole, in some non-Marxist work on discourse practice is focused on what seems local and immediate – in the university, the prison, the hospital or the factory.

There is, Foucault suggests, a connection between this concept of practice and a series of resistances which, like that in education, have developed in recent years: the resistances of women, of gays, of the psychiatrized, and of prisoners;

challenges to the power of medicine over the population, and of administration, with its regulations and secret files (1982, p. 211). In fact, work on discourse connects with these resistances in several ways, and perhaps most clearly in the ways in which it has problematized the twofold idea of individuality and sameness: the idea that we are all free individuals who speak the same language, hold the same values and know the same truths – unless, that is, we are aberrant and abnormal.

These resistances have developed in various countries: Britain, France, America. Foucault points out that these, unlike class struggles, are not necessarily concerned with 'forms of exploitation', nor, unlike racial and religious struggles, need they be concerned with 'forms of domination' (1982, p. 212). However, like class and racial struggles, they engage with ideological practices and, indeed, may be concerned exclusively with such practices. They are specifically directed against 'subjection, against forms of subjectivity and submission' (p. 212).

They challenge whatever breaks links and groupings, whatever individualizes a population by tying each to an identity, a function, a place, turning each in upon herself or himself; and they assert the right to be different (pp. 211–12). As such, they are resistances to what can be called 'humanism'. They often take issue with those discourses and practices which announce that submission to a 'norm' confers individuality and freedom: '"the more you submit to those in power, then the more this increases your [individual] sovereignty"' (Foucault 1971b, coll. 1977a, p. 221). But they do not take issue only with what humanism announces; it is not merely attitudes that they wish to change. They are resistances to the discourses of humanism, its techniques and forms of power, its knowledges, its institutional effects. The 'government of individualization' (Foucault 1982, p. 212) – the practices and discourses which regulate and construct individuals – is called into question by them. Recent work has connected with them in several respects, not least in refusing the idea of a norm of language and looking instead to discourses. Furthermore, it has turned to the history of humanist practices, discourses and knowledges: in this way, some of Foucault's studies have patiently dismantled the means used by the 'government of individualization'.

The resistances of women, of gays and of others, as Foucault outlines them, are libertarian, within bourgeois politics. They aim to change ideological practices and the effects of power linked to discourse, without being particularly concerned about basic economic relations or looking to build socialism.

But there are other struggles belonging to those whom Foucault mentions, perhaps to women particularly, which have a different and egalitarian aim, outside bourgeois politics. These seek to change, in addition to ideological practices, the economic relations, because women and men cannot be equal where women themselves are unequal and men too. These egalitarian struggles also, but differently, take issue with 'humanism' (besides other bourgeois themes), both for its subjective unpleasantness and for the way it disarms women and men in the labour movement. For humanism, in its insistence on sameness and individuality, acts as a means of forgetting, in the first place, that inequality is at the basis of the society in which we live. It therefore forgets the struggle of the mass of women and men who are wage-earners and whose struggle is ultimately a class struggle against both exploitation and those ideologies and discourses which help to ensure that exploitation continues.

In the PCF in May 1968, the effect of humanism was precisely to disarm women and men. A number of humanist and related bourgeois themes and practices had found a way into the PCF, and continue there, displacing Marxist theory. Instead of following the Marxist line that the masses make history, the PCF line in 1968 was that the Party in the person of its leaders and 'experts' makes history. Inflexible, underestimating the masses, the PCF acted to separate rather than weld together the various – worker, student and petty-bourgeois – forces. In 'What Must Change in the Party', Althusser points out that already at the end of the sixties the PCF was tending to become much too at home in bourgeois politics, 'a party like the rest' (1978, trans. 1978, p. 30).

It has been, in part, in relation to the stand taken in respect of the PCF that the work on discourse coming out of France since the sixties (for example, the work of Foucault, Althusser and Pêcheux) has developed along lines which on occasions diverge from each other. Some work, noticeably Foucault's, through a total refusal of the PCF, has been at times ambiguous in its politics and run the risk in countering one bourgeois theme, such as humanism, of slipping back into another, becoming pragmatic or subjective, and never fully breaking with bourgeois politics. Politically, the work of Althusser and Pêcheux is less ambiguous. From a development of Marxist positions, it has been an intervention within the PCF, criticizing the way the PCF has been infiltrated by bourgeois practices and discourses, by humanism, indeed, but also by pragmatism. But its main advances cannot be regarded as narrow interventions in one party, even if they have some of their determinants there. For this work has opened up the study of ideologies and discourses in new ways. While it raises questions about the neutrality of knowledges, about the concept of a norm of language, about how individuals are constructed as subjects (questions that are taken up a little differently in Foucault's work), it turns specifically to the ways in which ideological practices, discourses and their meanings exist historically and materially, what effects they have and how they may be changed.

May 1968, in the university, questioned not only knowledge and the curriculum, but also the forms of regulation and individualization within the university: examination procedures, segregation in the halls of residence; the disciplines that define knowledges and students; the division of students from the broad mass of working people. Since the sixties, in Britain as in other countries, there have been continuing challenges in tertiary education to examination procedures and disciplinary boundaries. There have also been struggles to teach outside humanist (and all ultimately idealist) discourses and practices, and outside the humanist knowledges, such as English Literature, psychology and so forth.

In Britain, work on discourse has primarily been developed where one aspect or another of the 'crisis' in education has made it possible to question powerful knowledges. First, in the seventies, there was a breakdown of social-democratic policy. Whether from within or to the right of the Labour Party, the 'failure' of educational expansion and comprehensive schooling to produce what their proponents had claimed they would – an equal or, at least, more equal society – was used to cast doubt on 'expansion', 'progressive methods' and 'teacher autonomy', all of which had been Labour Party policy (see Finn et al. 1978). It was here that some intellectuals began to consider that 'the reasons for this lack of success should be sought in the specific political location of schooling' (p. 189). The neutrality of knowledge and education was called into question.

Another, and an important, part of the educational context in Britain at this time was the tendency of the prevailing discourses and knowledges to disallow the psychoanalytical, post-structuralist and Marxist theories which were then being imported into the country. The refusal, in many parts of tertiary education, to allow these theories to be taught to students effectively posed, for those who wished to teach them, questions of the politics of knowledge and the status of discourses.

Work on discourse, then, is itself not neutral. The questions it poses concerning the historical and material existence of ideologies, discourses and their meanings, concerning the ways in which individuals are constructed as subjects, and concerning the relations between theory and practice involved in 'speaking for others', are questions that some would prefer never to raise. For there stand, behind the work on discourse that emerged and developed at the end of the sixties and in the seventies, the ultimately political questions of how and how far the society in which we live can be changed.

2

From ideology to discourse: the Althusserian stand

Even before 1968, meanings were not always and all considered neutral. Uneasy distinctions were in force: to claim some meanings as neutral and true, others were branded biased and illusory. But more recently, in the work on discourse that has come to question meanings in their material and social construction, the politics of the range of meanings has been made available to analysis. This has required a departure from the view of language as a system of meanings shared by all. So Pêcheux has stated that 'words, expressions, propositions, etc., change their meaning according to the positions held by those who use them' (1975, trans. 1982, p. 111). Pêcheux's thesis, which directs us to the politics of meaning in conflicting discourses, takes its cue from the radical breakthrough in the understanding of ideologies provided by Althusser's 1970 essay on 'Ideology and Ideological State Apparatuses (Notes towards an Investigation)'. Before turning to that breakthrough, I will use some writings of the period 1790 to 1830 to illustrate a part of what Pêcheux's thesis suggests.

In England at that time, the established church was opposed by both 'atheists' and dissenting organizations. Within those conflicts – linked to class in the last instance – words were a weapon of struggle so that, for example, what might count as a 'hymn' became an issue of some importance. Shelley's *Hymn to Intellectual Beauty* (1817) was not published to be sung in a congregation, but as a poem, a piece of writing for an individual to read in solitude. This 'hymn' used words from the standard vocabulary of orthodox Christianity ('grace', 'spirit', 'love', 'hope', etc.), but it set them in phrases where they could take their meaning from unorthodox positions:

> Love, Hope, and Self-esteem, like clouds depart
> And come, for some uncertain moments lent.
> Man were immortal, and omnipotent,
> Didst thou, unknown and awful as thou art,
> Keep with thy glorious train firm state within his heart.

In these lines, love and hope, immortality and omnipotence, are connected with arguments about man and the individual self. These words, in effect, were brought down to earth, and in this way could take their meanings from 'atheist' and humanist positions.

Another example: the word 'salvation'. By reference to differing positions between the established church and dissenting organizations, that word found differing meanings. According to the Anglican missionary hymn, 'From Greenland's icy mountains' (1819), 'salvation' consisted in gaining eternal life through faith in Christ:

> The heathen in his blindness
> Bows down to wood and stone:
>
> Shall we, whose souls are lighted
> With wisdom from on high:
> Shall we to men benighted
> The lamp of life deny?
> Salvation! O salvation!
> The joyful sound proclaim,
> Till each remotest nation
> Has learnt Messiah's name!

But in dissenting writings, both hymns and sermons, 'salvation' was brought to consist in freedom from despotic rule. Richard Price's sermon addressed to Protestant dissenters in the Revolution Society, and printed in 1790, incorporated Simeon's speech from Luke (part of Evensong in the Anglican Church) into a panegyric on the revolution in France:

> *Lord now lettest thou thy servant depart in peace, for mine eyes have seen thy salvation.* I have lived to see a diffusion of knowledge, which has undermined superstition and error – I have lived to see the rights of men better understood than ever; and nations panting for liberty, which seemed to have lost the idea of it. – I have lived to see THIRTY MILLIONS of people, indignant and resolute, spurning at slavery, and demanding liberty with an irresistible voice; their king led in triumph, and an arbitrary monarch surrendering himself to his subjects. (Price 1790, p. 49)

The hymn 'O God of Hosts, Thine ear incline', written to be sung at a meeting of the 'Friends of Peace and Reform', was still in 1794 waiting for God to give 'salvation' in that same dissenting sense:

> Mad tyrants tame, break down the high
> Whose haughty foreheads beat the sky,
>
> Make bare Thine arm, great King of Kings!
> That arm alone salvation brings:
> That wonder-working arm which broke
> From Israel's neck the Egyptian yoke.
>
> Burst every dungeon, every chain!
> Give injured slaves their rights again.

The words 'hymn' and 'salvation' were weapons of struggle; to return to Pêcheux's thesis, words 'change their meaning according to the positions held by those who use them' (1975, trans. 1982, p. 111).

This thesis, which points out the antagonism of verbal meanings, follows on (as has been said) from Althusser's breakthrough in the wider understanding of ideologies – the beliefs, meanings and practices in which we think and act. Earlier attempts to link those beliefs and practices to the historical process had tended to be reductive. They had tried to connect discrepant categories, ideas in the mind (on the one hand) and the technical side of the economy (on the other), as if meanings and beliefs could at the same time reflect reality and be formed in consciousness, whether a true or a false consciousness. Such an approach to ideology supposes that ideas have an abstract existence and are shaped by consciousness. As a result, it overlooks much of the politics of meaning.[1]

Althusser's essay of 1970 reorientated the study of ideology by emphasizing that ideologies have, first of all, a material existence. It gives an approximate list of 'apparatuses' (i.e. institutions), in contemporary capitalist countries such as France or Britain, whose operations are largely ideological: the apparatuses of religion, education, the family, the law, the system of party politics, the trade unions, communications and culture (1970, coll. 1971, pp. 136–7). The thrust of the argument is that ideologies exist in apparatuses forming part of the State, where they are 'unified' or, we might say, interconnected by the social and, ultimately, class conflicts, traversing those apparatuses. The argument escapes the abstract view of beliefs and meanings as either free-floating or coming from consciousness. Quite differently, Althusser holds that consciousness is constructed through ideologies, and his radical emphasis on their material existence leads to this reconception: ideologies are systems of meanings that install everybody in imaginary relations to the real relations in which they live (pp. 152–5).

In France, the essay has underpinned work by Pêcheux, Renée Balibar, Étienne Balibar, Macherey and Foucault. Althusser never offered this essay as definitive: 'This text is made up of two extracts from an ongoing study' (p. 123). Whereas the first half has as an object the existence of ideologies and ideological State apparatuses (hereafter, ISAs) under capitalism, the second half concerns ideology in general and as such is wholly philosophical. But outside France, inattention to this difference (and a tendency to read backwards from the second half) has often confused and obscured the importance of the essay.

Its vital importance seems to me that it opens the road to a knowledge (which does not claim to be perfect and pure) of how ideologies and discourses are set up and what effects they have. In its first half, the essay indicates that ideologies not only come from social conflicts but also, in the prevailing practices of ideology, reimpose those conflicts. In short, the ISAs are the site of a double struggle. Althusser's argument and point of view can be followed most readily by considering first, as he does, what is reimposed.

The prevailing practices

Althusser begins by suggesting that an investigation of ideologies start from the 'point of view of reproduction'. Referring to a letter from Marx to Kugelmann, he writes, 'every child knows that a social formation which did not reproduce the conditions of production at the same time as it produced would not last a year' (p. 123). In this, he is working directly within Marx's analysis of capitalist society as a class society in which the basic relations of production are relations of exploitation. Marx's analysis of capitalism laid out how wage-earners to support themselves are obliged to sell their labour power, and through their 'surplus' (i.e. unpaid) labour generate the capital which reproduces their exploitation: 'The ownership of past unpaid labour is thenceforth the sole condition for the appropriation of living unpaid labour on a constantly increasing scale' (1867, trans. 1976, p. 729). Starting from reproduction, Althusser is starting from class struggle between the bourgeoisie and the proletariat – for this antagonism is reproduced along with the capital-labour relation within production. Even though he is quick to point out that labour power in the form of a skilled work-force is reproduced largely 'outside the firm' in the family and at school (1970, coll. 1971, pp. 126–7), the reproduction of capitalist relations takes place within production itself. But in looking only within production, Marx left certain questions unasked – not least, how social division is imposed from outside the factory or the firm, how workers 'accept' their exploitation, how it is secured (or, conversely, not secured). It is to tackle the question, 'how is the reproduction of the relations of production secured?' (p. 141) that Althusser comes to take the ideological level as a set of State apparatuses.

To give substance to Althusser's theoretical argument, in the course of this chapter, I will turn to the example of education, which Althusser indicates as occupying the key place among the State apparatuses in mature capitalist societies (pp. 144–5). The ruling body of the bourgeoisie, brought to power in the French Revolution, wrote into the Declaration of Rights of the new republic of 1793 that 'Education is a necessity for all' (quoted in Soboul 1962, trans. 1974, II, p. 315). But what this amounted to in nineteenth-century practices, both in France and in England, was the establishment of primary schooling for everyone, alongside the elite secondary system already in existence. In mature capitalist societies, while education is compulsory, it is not the same for all: education is divisive. The Butler Act of 1944, which provided for secondary education for all in post-war Britain, was again divisive while claiming to be egalitarian: pushing most children into secondary modern and technical schools, selecting some for the grammar schools.[2] In Thatcherite Britain, where a division is most visible in the split between comprehensives and public-independent schools, the division is currently being reinforced through the extension of education to give, on the one hand, formal higher education and, on the other, training schemes reabsorbed into the work-place. But Althusser's argument draws attention to more than this, being concerned not just with where people learn but with what they learn.

His argument is that 'ruling ideology' secures the reproduction of capitalist relations through the instituting of social division. In schools, children learning skills acquire 'a certain amount of "know-how" wrapped in the ruling ideology (French, arithmetic, natural history, the sciences, literature) or simply the ruling ideology in its pure state (ethics, civic instruction, philosophy)' (1970, coll. 1971, p. 147). And yet, crucially, children learn 'know-how' under forms which not only subject them to ruling ideology but also institute a division so that for many there is 'submission to the ruling ideology', linked to incomprehension, and for others there is mastery, an 'ability to manipulate' its devices (pp. 127–8). It is therefore all too true that, as Pêcheux said, many 'undergo their schooling as an imposition, a bad period to be got over as soon as possible' (1975, trans. 1982, pp. 164–5).

A clear instance, from the 'content' of teaching, of how the prevailing ideology divides while appearing to do otherwise, is available from Renée Balibar's study of the teaching of grammar. For her, Althusser's interventions 'have opened the road to research' (Balibar 1974, p. 54); and she has put them to use in her many studies of French national language and literature. One paper on the teaching of grammar (which has been translated into English) details the history of its imposed division from the French Revolution when, in 1794, the ruling middle class chose the French half of a dual French-Latin grammar as a State grammar for the instruction of all

(1978, pp. 30–7). This led to a system in which the primary-school pupil learnt – and still learns – the national language under the form of a grammar largely meaningless in the absence of instruction in Latin. All children could be given a mechanical understanding of 'correct French', thereby facilitating communication. But what was taught in primary schools could be broken down and rebuilt in secondary schooling, with some children being given a mastery of 'correct French', a mastery that would bring about a form of non-communication by obliterating what had been learnt before and by all. For the choice of the French half of a dual grammar as the State grammar

> resulted in the study of comparative grammar – and thus a full understanding of the generative schema of the national language – being restricted to the secondary level of education, which had been envisaged from the start as multilingual (and above all bilingual – French and Latin) in character. Orwell's famous saying comes to mind in this connection: 'All citizens are equal, but some are more equal than others.' (p. 32)

Like her more extensive studies of education in post-revolutionary France, this paper gives specificity to Althusser's broader argument. Its historical research exposes the ways in which a national system of education can be a means of subjecting all within a divisive relation imposing submission and granting mastery.

Now, the interest of this to me is that, while suggesting why prevailing practices need to be changed, the argument begins to indicate how they operate installed in dominance in apparatuses. Althusser may well be correct to call these apparatuses of the State (alongside the repressive apparatus of government, administration and the police, the courts, the army). For he takes it that the ruling class moves to exercise its hegemony over and in the ISAs (1970, coll. 1971, pp. 136–9). Here he is building on Gramsci's 'remarkable' intuition that the State is not simply a 'coercive apparatus' but can work with velvet gloves through supposedly civilizing apparatuses by means of which 'the hegemony of one social group over the entire nation' is exercised (Gramsci, letter of 7 September 1931, trans. 1979, p. 204). Through the ISAs, ruling ideology by subjecting and dividing helps secure (shielded by the repressive State apparatus) the reproduction of those capitalist relations of production on which is based the social and political dominance of the bourgeoisie (Althusser 1970, coll. 1971, pp. 136–42).

But this is not all: Althusser's argument suggests something else which seems to me to have a primary importance. It indicates how, 'before' this, the prevailing practices of ideology become such, and how ideologies are constructed. Now, whatever might have been said during the years of the French Revolution, if we give even a little attention to historical struggles, it is clear that the bourgeoisie does not exercise its control over the ISAs by some necessary or natural right. Althusser points out that the bourgeoisie, for all its concentrated attacks on the church (the key ISA in the pre-capitalist period), neither subordinated the church overnight nor immediately wrested its ideological functions away from it to install education as the key apparatus (pp. 143–5). It would be a mistake to think that the installation in dominance of ruling ideology happens all by itself. 'On the contrary', he argues, 'it is the stake in a very bitter and continuous class struggle: first against the former ruling classes and their positions in the old and new ISAs, then against the exploited class'. He adds that this struggle goes beyond the ISAs, for 'it comes from elsewhere', being rooted ultimately in the relations of production themselves (p. 172).

Ideologies in struggle

The preceding section has taken up Althusser's account of how the prevailing practices of ideology impose divisively on everyone. But to consider only this would make it seem as if ruling ideology is all there is, with no means of change. Happily, Althusser's position in the essay takes us out of such grim determinism.

Starting from reproduction, Althusser is, as already mentioned, starting from struggle – from class struggle. From this, he is led to consider something more than ruling ideology and how it acts divisively and imposes beliefs, etc., upon those it subordinates as if what is imposed were their beliefs, their abilities or their culture. He is led to take account of ruled ideologies as well. Many earlier theories, while not ignoring these, had been waylaid by thinking of different ideologies as expressing the subjective consciousness of the different classes. Althusser's position seems to me to make a key advance in getting things much more in their real material order, in starting from class struggle rather than from the classes themselves. From this, he can argue that ideologies are set up in what are ultimately antagonistic relations: no ideology takes shape outside a struggle with some opposing ideology. It is this argument which has provided the cue for the kind of work on discourse which was sketched at the start of this chapter and will be developed in the next.

The breakthrough made by Althusser's argument becomes evident when we consider what he calls the 'unity' of the ISAs. Those apparatuses he lists are not particularly discrete. For example, in modern capitalist societies, there are interactions between the system of political parties, the law and the trade unions. Likewise, education and culture interact so that some ideological forms are constructed between them. (Literature, in the way it has been set up since the last century, is a case in point.) None the less, Althusser emphasizes, the ISAs are not an 'organized whole' like the repressive State apparatus (p. 141). Certainly, as the history of the trade unions indicates, there is nothing to say that ruling ideology is always dominant in each. Even looking only at ruling ideology in the ISAs, we can see that it has no necessary homogeneity. If the ISAs are unified, it cannot be in some identity.

What Althusser proposes is that 'the ideology by which they function is always in fact unified, despite its diversity and contradictions, *beneath the ruling ideology*' (p. 139). That is to say, ruling and ruled ideologies – while having determinants outside the ISAs and so, he states, 'not "born" in the ISAs' (p. 173) – do not come together as unconnected units, but take shape in relation to each other, antagonistically (under the dominance of ruling ideology). Formed as means of domination and resistance, ideologies are never simply free to set their own terms but are marked by what they are opposing. Pêcheux clarifies further by saying that ideological struggle is not 'the meeting point of two distinct and pre-existing worlds' (1975, trans. 1982, p. 98).

While Althusser's proposition that the ISAs are unified has been read in other ways so as to turn him into a 'functionalist', that is missing the point.[3] It is in defining the unity of what we may call 'uneven contradiction', by which ideologies in the ISAs take shape, that his working principle advances the study of ideology and discourse. And, in the next chapter, I will explain more fully how it has been put to work in the study of discourse.

Let me, first, spell out the proposition more fully. Implicit in it is a denial that ideologies take shape in consciousness. In their class links, ideologies do not express the habits of thought of a class, its world outlook. They emerge, so to speak, from between the classes and are linked to a class as its ideological means of control or come-back. So what he argues is that the ISAs provide an 'objective field to contradictions which express, in forms which may be limited or extreme, the effects of the clashes between the capitalist class struggle and the proletarian class struggle, as well as their subordinate forms' (1970, coll. 1971, pp. 141–2).

This helps us to grasp the important point that the ideology locally dominant in an ISA comes from a position in struggle, it is pinned down where it acts as a weapon, and it is reshaped through struggles. And this is to say that an ideology, however dominant it may be in an ISA, does not exist without some opposing ideology and that opposing ideologies are shaped by each other.

This argument seems to me to offer suggestions not just for research but for political practice. What it suggests is that the ISAs recurrently 'may be not only the *stake*, but also the *site* of class struggle' (p. 140); and the struggle is double. Again, education can be considered as an example. In education, resistance has come to be set both against the dominance of ruling ideology (to install in education other practices and knowledges), and against the divisiveness it imposes. Even so, if the ISAs are not discrete units, it would be a mistake to think that what's at stake is simply the apparatuses that exist and the ideologies that are dominant in each. Althusser's discussion of how, in mature capitalist societies, education has been installed in key place, displacing the church, makes plain how what's at stake can be not only or even primarily what ideology is to be institutionally dominant, but the relations between the ISAs. In various capitalist countries, there is some form of simultaneous affiliation of the trade-union ISA and non-affiliation of the educational ISA to party politics. Because of this, a prevailing impression can be given that, on the one hand, trade unions are represented by and hence rightly sub-ordinated to the national government and, on the other hand, education is neutral. Change and resistance here (in the disturbances around the educational apparatus in western countries over the past 15–20 years) have involved attempts to reorder, to bring education into relation with quite other practices of politics than those which currently prevail.

Althusser's theorizing of the ISAs was offered, modestly, as 'notes towards an investigation' which need, and have begun to be put to use. These notes do not cover everything, and make little reference to ideological struggles that are not in the first instance along class lines and bear upon gender or race. To foreground these requires a development of the theory, so as to indicate, for example, how prevailing practices by subordinating women promote a gendered resistance. Indeed, given the principle that, while ideologies take shape antagonistically (under the dominance of ruling ideology), ruling ideology can operate divisively, granting mastery and imposing submission, it should be possible to analyse the historical, including current, relations between ideologies that come from positions of race or gender as well as from class positions.

From this basis, it is only a short step to the analysis of discourses in their meaningful antagonisms. But first some problems which would otherwise intrude must be overcome. For it is increasingly clear that ideological beliefs and practices cannot have, as humanism has claimed, a subjective source. The second half of Althusser's essay moves against humanist assumptions. Its arguments make considerable sense and yet, through not breaking completely with humanism, leave certain pitfalls. Avoiding these, we may come to the conclusion that there can be no general theory of ourselves as subjects.

Against humanism: problems of the subject

The argument I have outlined thus far from the first part of the essay on the ISAs makes proposals for research into existing ideologies. The second part differs from this: it was written as an intervention both in politics and in philosophy, moving against various effects of humanism in both. Pêcheux has described it as challenging specifically the 'narcissism of the organizations of the labour movement – the communist organizations in front – which had installed themselves like sleep-walkers within the psychological humanism of "conscience", of "becoming conscious", and of pedagogical progress' (1983, p. 32). An all too bourgeois humanism, recurrently, has infiltrated parts of the labour movement, and there it has imposed a set of assumptions about 'human nature' and 'human freedom' which take it that Man, generally and individually, is the source of knowledge, meaning, history. History, then, is said to result from the action of a *subject*, who is Man, and, as Althusser points out, the thesis is put forward that 'It is man who makes history' (1973, coll. 1976b, p. 40). Such a thesis prevents any scientific investigation of history, while its political effect is to disarm men and women in the labour movement, and other women as well. Humanism (while belonging to bourgeois philosophy as a detachment of various prevailing ideologies) had, and still has, acquired a grip in the theory and practice of the French Communist Party. The second half of the ISAs essay moves sharply against humanist assumptions concerning Man as subject which present themselves as the common sense of what 'everyone knows'. In taking issue here with humanism, Althusser's philosophy makes the sense it does.

His philosophy engages through its address and, in doing so, provides a theory of how 'the "obviousness" that you and I are subjects – and that that does not cause any problems – is an ideological effect, the elementary ideological effect' (1970, coll. 1971, p. 161).[4] His argument is that we exist as subjects only in ideology, constituted there as subjects in a double sense: (a) held to be responsible, centres of initiative, through being (b) subjected and tied to an imaginary identity (p. 169). That is to say, ideology installs each of us in an imaginary relation to real relations. And the relation is imaginary because it works through recognition and identification to hail individuals into place. Althusser's central thesis is that

'Ideology interpellates individuals as subjects' and that it hails or interpellates them all: there is no escaping ideological subjection (pp. 160, 163).

From a story, included in the essay, of the policeman's hail – 'Hey, you there!' – we can begin to see what this thesis means:

> *interpellation* . . . can be imagined along the lines of the most commonplace everyday police (or other) hailing: 'Hey, you there!' . . . The hailed individual will turn round. By this mere one-hundred-and-eighty-degree physical conversion, he becomes a *subject*. Why? Because he has recognized that the hail was 'really' addressed to him, and that 'it was *really him* who was hailed' (and not someone else). (p. 163)

This story is presented in the essay to show how every ideology, through the mechanism of recognition, calls individuals into place and confers on them 'their' identity: ideology is addressed to individuals so that – answering, turning round, converted – they become 'freely' subjected to it. As a story, its one flaw is that it could imply that recognition comes from the individual. This could be corrected, however, by taking the case of somebody who turns round, 'knowing' the police have hailed him wrongly, and is arrested, or the situation of women at Greenham Common in Britain, refusing the installation of cruise missiles, and called by the law to 'recognize' themselves as committing criminal damage.

The crux of the argument is that we cannot get outside ideology. Our consciousness is constructed under the form of an imaginary subjection. In the apparatuses of ideology, in their day-to-day practices, we become particular individuals acting in the beliefs given us to think. Althusser cites a formula by Pascal which, almost taking note of this, 'says more or less: "Kneel down, move your lips in prayer, and you will believe"' (p. 158).

As a means of emphasizing that our consciousness is constructed and that we are not the free centres of initiative humanism supposes, Althusser's critique has been most useful. Even so, it stops slightly short. Like many critiques, his gives too much credence to the very assumptions it challenges, so that these set the limits of his philosophy: to displace the myth of an essential human nature, he lays before us a single and general mechanism of all ideology.

Now, it seems to me that Althusser's critique connects only in part with the remarkable advances made in the first half of the ISAs essay. Those advances were made by starting from class struggle, so as to grasp precisely that there really is no ideology-in-general and that what exists are ideologies set up through their antagonisms with each other. It may be the case, as Althusser has since argued, that a 'minimum of non-existent generality' is needed to perceive and understand what does exist (1975, coll. 1976b, p. 189). And in so much as it reorders and follows a material order, his thesis about 'interpellation' does begin to supply this: it stakes out that ideological subjection comes before and brings about the creation of ourselves as subjects. But where it stops short is in positing only a single mechanism of recognition, or of identification, in all ideology. That notion of a single mechanism can make us blind to what, even in the setting up of ideologies, is, I would argue, most material: contradiction, and thereby struggle. That notion risks taking us out of history and making change and revolt unthinkable.

To think ahead and out of this difficulty, the concept of 'disidentification', used by Pêcheux, is most helpful. Pêcheux sketches three mechanisms through which subjects may be constructed. Identification is the mode of 'good subjects', those who 'freely consent' to the image held out to them while 'bad subjects', trouble-makers, refuse it. Counter-identification is the mode of the trouble-maker who turns back those meanings 'lived' by the good subjects who are only stating the obvious – '"*what you call* the oil crisis", "*your* social sciences", "*your* Virgin Mary"' (1975, trans. 1982, pp. 156–7). These two modes have, he suggests, a ready 'symmetry' and in effect support each other. But aside from both these, he posits a third: 'disidentification', which can be described as an effect of working 'on and against' prevailing practices of ideological subjection (pp. 159, 215).

Even these differences, sketched by Pêcheux, may seem rather general. They need to be specified more precisely in relation to ruling ideological practices (of the law, of schooling, where assessment and examinations are considered, with compelling irony, educational) which continue to dominate us and do indeed insist on us as free, responsible subjects each owning before anything else 'his' own identity. Counter-identification can then be understood to come from a rejection of this identity that remains complicit with it. Disidentification, by contrast, comes from another position, one existing antagonistically, with the effect that the identity and identifications set up in dominant ideology, though never escaped entirely, are transformed and displaced. In other words, a disidentification can be brought about by political and ideological practices which work on and against what prevails. Even a theory such as Pêcheux's can have something of this effect. Further instances of what is at stake here are developed in chapters 4 and 6.

From this argument, we can have a sharper sense of what is amiss in the notion of a single and general mechanism. If ideologies simply effected identifications, then resistance at this level (were it there at all) could be only the outcome of a differing identification, as if ruling and ruled ideologies existed separately rather as two football teams exist separately before a match – that analogy is cited and firmly opposed in Althusser's later writing (1973, coll. 1976b, p. 49). It is the antagonistic existence of ideologies which for a moment had been forgotten in the earlier philosophy of ideology with its one general mechanism. Ideology (singular and general) is out of place in the history of class societies. And so is 'the subject'.

Not seeing this, work of the seventies often took the ISAs essay to task for giving no complete theory of the subject. The essay was criticized or rethought to compensate for the supposed defects of not properly assimilating the unconscious from psychoanalysis and the speaking subject from linguistics. It was asked to supply a theory of subjectivity.[5] Film and literary criticism using the essay as a springboard tried to jump to the spectator/reader as a subject constructed through the ideological mechanism of the text. Texts were analysed, and even graded, according to the consistency or otherwise with which 'the subject' was constructed.[6] The mistake in these projects came not only from holding onto some substantive notion of human consciousness, as Stuart Hall pointed out early on (1978, p. 118), which Althusser's concern with ideological subjection – 'There are no subjects except by and for their subjection' (1970, coll. 1971, p. 169) – was there to displace. It came also from the second half of the essay which, in positing a general form of subjection, goes too far towards supposing that as subjects constituted in ideology all are, and always will have been, the same. That philosophy, in countering humanist assumptions, remains too reliant on them.

In some ways, then, the second part of the ISAs essay is at odds with the first, which makes its advances through refocusing attention on existing ideologies. It seems that if research on subjection is also to advance this will be through analysing existing forms. Others may well take further Pêcheux's brief work on two dominant forms of ideological subjection under capitalism, which he calls the 'American' and 'Prussian' ways (see 1983, pp. 33–5). Foucault's studies of bourgeois subjection – the 'government of individualization' (discussed in chapter 6) – are perhaps more exemplary. But if advances are to be made in this area, work on subjection cannot afford to forget dominated ideologies and disidentification. Meanwhile, it would seem that attempts to supply a theory of the subject (singular and general) for ideology or discourse will tend to idealism, speculating about what does not exist.

3

Meaningful antagonisms: Pêcheux on discourse

The essay on the ISAs is directed towards ideological practices. At the same time, it provides the cue for a questioning of discourses that are specifically verbal: words and phrases as they are used in everyday speech or in serious writings. Through a development of Althusser's theory, we can consider how discourses are set up and the politics (one might say) of their words and meanings. A path to take here is indicated by the theory of how ideologies exist antagonistically.

It is a path followed, at least at times, in Pêcheux's *Language, Semantics and Ideology* (1975, trans. 1982). His work explores the relations which discourses have, on the one hand, with ideological practices and, on the other, with the language which is supposedly shared by all. By exploring those relations, his work suggests that discourses are not at all peaceful; they develop out of clashes with one another, and because of this there is a political dimension to each use of words and phrases in writing or in speech.

Before taking up these issues from his work, I will mention, to clear out of the way, some problems that there are with parts of *Language, Semantics and Ideology*, for it is an uneven book. Some of the arguments head in quite a different direction from the main path and become caught up in undue generalities where theory of the subject forms the centre. These problems are effects of how the book was written within 'the kind of "Triple Alliance"' concluded 'between the names of Althusser, Lacan and Saussure' (Pêcheux 1982, coll. 1982, p. 211). In the seventies, that alliance often seemed 'only too convenient' for the traffic of theories; but 'something was wrong', as Pêcheux's postscript points out (p. 211). Both structural linguistics (Saussure) and psychoanalysis (Lacan), in different ways, posited general mechanisms: of the system of language and the unconscious. Parts of Pêcheux's book combine these with the second half of Althusser's essay and its general mechanism of interpellation (and in so doing forget about disidentification). This seems to me mistaken, tending to idealism (nobody is perfect). But leaving these aside, let us see how the real advances are made in Pêcheux's theory.

First of all, by going over to materialist positions, his theory dispenses with the kind of semantics which looks for universal meanings. A prevailing interest in universal semantics has imposed itself on many linguists, among them the Polish linguist, Adam Schaff. Pêcheux questions it. According to the dictionaries followed by Schaff, semantics is 'a branch of linguistics . . . concerned with the meaning and changes of meaning of words and expressions' (quoted in Pêcheux 1975, trans. 1982, p. 2). As such, it might seem of major importance to anyone working on discourse; unless, and this is the contention Pêcheux takes up and develops, words do not have their own meaning, a universal meaning which may change only at intervals.

Current semantics provides more of an obstacle than an aid to investigations of how meanings have been socially constructed, and Pêcheux's arguments alert us to the problems. Through a historical survey, he indicates how semantics, unlike the study of signifying sounds or of syntax, has come to form a point of entry through which traditional philosophy continues to entrap linguistics (pp. 21–33. The trap is laid by the assumption that meanings have both an 'ideal' and a 'subjective' status: as if, on the one hand, there is something rather like a pure logic of ideas which might be used to give knowledge of things and, on the other, a rhetoric of the concrete and the everyday which might express a speaker's subjective situation (pp. 37–40). That assumption, he argues, 'forgets' existing sciences, either reducing 'science' to 'logical reasoning' or marketing 'science' as a 'game' (pp. 45–6). Secondly, it makes the changes of words and meanings impossible to consider outside the vague commonplaces that 'social factors' and 'individual creativity' influence the language. By going over to materialist positions, and thus departing from the traditional view, Pêcheux can recall the existence of the sciences. And he can take up the political dimension of the meaning of words in discourses.

Discourse and position

To consider the politics of meaning, we need to let go, then, of the notion that words have a meaning of their own, one pinned down for everyone alike in the system of a language such as French or English. Something different has been sketched at the start of the previous chapter: words change their meaning from one discourse to another, and conflicting discourses develop even where there is a supposedly common language. Arguing this, Pêcheux considers that it is not the language which determines the meanings of words and phrases in discourses: the real 'exterior' of those meanings has 'nothing at all to do with purely linguistic properties' (p. 185). Indeed, meanings are part of the 'ideological sphere' and discourse is one of ideology's specific forms.

Here his argument follows from the essay on the ISAs. In so doing, it takes the line that the meanings of discourses are set up in what are ultimately antagonistic relations – in struggles which cut across the apparatuses of ideology, and which, if not immediately, are in the end linked to 'class struggle in its various economic, political and ideological forms'. These struggles are the 'exterior' which sets up discursive meanings (pp. 185–6). Like Althusser, Pêcheux places the emphasis on struggles of class, and his method here, like Althusser's, is in no way reductive. Moreover, his approach is a vital step forward from structuralism in the sixties. Structuralist arguments, it seems to me, were unable to come any nearer to real material determinants of meaning than by invoking a signifying code in the language and then calling this, in a quick turnabout, 'material'.

How does struggle, when conducted in the ideological sphere, bear upon discourse? It may be useful to consider some examples. The discourses in which we think have an 'obvious' specialization into distinct areas: they may be part of religion, part of educational knowledge, part of culture, etc. But let us not be trapped by the obvious into supposing that discourses have natural boundaries and are born, one by one, each in a single institution. In schools, discourse of a religious character is often used and its placing there tends both to mask and to endorse dominant educational practices – such discourse is, in effect, as much a part of ruling-class weaponry in the school as in the church. At times, however, and with a quite different effect, some of the discourse used in organizations of the labour movement may come within the church. During the miners' strike of 1984–5 in Britain, some Anglican bishops used vocabularies and arguments which were, in effect, on the side of the miners and of all who are exploited under capitalism. In the end, what matters most with a discourse, I would argue, is less in what institution it is used than the position it takes, the stand in struggle which, through its effects, it takes. It is not only in the relations within an institution but also – and perhaps this is the vital point – in the relations between and across institutions that there can be conflicting words and meanings.

To develop a theory of how discourses are constructed, Pêcheux proposes that ideological struggle traverses the 'whole' of discourse. In so doing, it disjoins 'thought' into various areas and specialisms and brings about shifting alignments among them (pp. 99–100, 185–6). Though it may seem unusual to consider discourse as a 'whole', this argument has the advantage of indicating how discourses, in contradiction, are related. For it points out that what is thought within one discourse is an effect related to what is unthought there but thought elsewhere in another. In this way, 'the unasserted precedes and dominates the assertion' (p. 187). This can clarify the instance of the word *salvation*, discussed in chapter 2, in the use made of that word in the Romantic period:

> Make bare Thine arm, great King of Kings!
> That arm alone salvation brings:
> That wonder-working arm which broke
> From Israel's neck the Egyptian yoke.
>
> Burst every dungeon, every chain!
> Give injured slaves their rights again.

What was 'unthought' as salvation for this hymn of religious and political dissent (namely, being saved through faith in Christ to life eternal) in part could determine the thought, within the hymn, of salvation as an immediate release from despotism. The thought, expressing a difference or a conflict, depends on the unthought.

In that case, discourse is not the individual's way of inhabiting the language, a kind of self-expression. The language takes on meaning and discourses are constructed through struggles.[1] Pêcheux's arguments, as already stated, stress that the 'material character' of meaning does not lie in its being determined by linguistic elements ('signifiers'). Nor does the meaning of a word exist 'in itself'. Instead, meaning exists antagonistically: it comes from positions in struggle, so that 'words ... change their meaning according to the positions' from which they are used (p. 111). And, as can be

seen by developing this further, such changes are unautho-
rized – no one casts a spell on the words. The positions, by
reference to which words find meaning, Pêcheux explains, are
ideological positions inscribed in the practices of class or
other struggles between and within apparatuses.

This explanation draws a line which separates materialist
study of discourses from a whole host of idealist themes. It
suggests how a discourse can be specified: first of all, by a
position in a given conjuncture and, second, by the institutional areas (religious, educational and so forth) to which the
discourse pertains. Indeed, going further, it points out that
the position and institutional siting together determine, at any
given stage in struggle, 'what can and should be said
(articulated in the form of a speech, a sermon, a pamphlet, a
report, a programme, etc.)' (p. 111).

Even so, the obvious line of thought might be to suppose
that such determinants can only act on and through the
speaker's subjective views. But, by keeping to a materialist
approach, Pêcheux's argument makes a further advance: it
suggests that these determinants act on and through the
ordering of words and expressions in discourse. How words
are used, what can be said, very much consists in how words
are put together so that they are synonymous with or
paraphrase each other, or connect metonymically with each
other in a discourse. It is these relationships into which one
word, expression or proposition enters with others of the
same discourse that Pêcheux calls a 'discursive process', a
process through which words take on meanings. And he
emphasizes that just as words can change their meaning from
one discourse to another, so within one discourse different
words can have the 'same' meaning, which is 'in fact the
condition for each element (word, expression or proposition)
having a meaning at all' (p. 112). What is at stake in discursive
struggles may well be this ordering and combining of words.

To characterize the effects which antagonistic positions
have had upon the combining of words in discourse we can
look at the words *liberty, rights* and *natural* as used in some

further English writings of the 1790s. The French Declaration of Rights of 1789 – a liberal bourgeois document of the Revolution — was 'translated' into English through Price's *A Discourse on the Love of our Country* (printed 1790) and through Part I of Paine's *Rights of Man* (printed 1791). All three of these documents were opposed by or to Burke's conservative and anti-revolutionary *Reflections on the Revolution in France* (printed 1790).[2] Between these various writings, the 'same' words *liberty*, *rights* and *natural* seem to have been a point of differentiation between two discourses which (in the politics of their struggle) were, the one, liberal revolutionary and, the other, conservative in position.

For the liberal bourgeois discourse, *liberty*, *rights* and *natural* were connected metonymically (each as a part of the others) and centred, so to speak, in their meanings on the 'equality' of 'man' and of 'the individual'. Here 'liberty' is part of what is 'natural':

1 *Liberty* is one of 'the chief blessings of human nature' (Price 1790, p. 11). As a 'natural right', it is one of 'the natural and imprescriptible rights of man' (Declaration of Rights, in Paine 1791, p. 111).
2 *Rights*, in being natural, are 'equal' (Price 1790, p. 21), for 'Men are born ... equal in respect of their rights' (Declaration of Rights, in Paine 1791, p. 111).
3 What is *natural* is what is human and individual: rights that are 'Natural ... appertain to man' from 'his existence' and are 'pre-existing in the individual' (Paine 1791, pp. 48–9).

In such ways, the three terms are bound to each other and to 'man' and 'the individual', in metonymic relations, while 'natural' and 'equal' are held together as near synonyms for each other.

For the conservative discourse, the three terms are again connected metonymically but in quite a different way: none of them appertains to 'man' in general. In the first place, 'liberties' (plural) are inherited:

1 'Our *liberties*' are 'an entailed inheritance'. They are inherited as privileges: 'We have an inheritable crown; an inheritable peerage; and an house of commons and a people inheriting privileges, franchises, and liberties' (Burke 1793, p. 47).

2 If 'liberties' here can be called by the name of *rights*, that is because 'rights' and 'privileges' are synonymous – 'our nature' and 'our breasts' are 'the great conservatories . . . of our rights and privileges' (p. 50).

3 This *natural* conservatory of rights is not the nature of man and the individual; instead, whatever is modelled on familial descent and nature's continuity is *natural*. That 'our liberties' are 'an entailed inheritance' is 'the happy effect of following nature', for it is by 'working after the pattern of nature' that 'we transmit . . . our privileges, in the same manner in which we enjoy and transmit our property and our lives', namely, as a 'family settlement' (pp. 47–8).

In such ways, words change their meanings.

The conservative discourse uses the 'same' three words and, moreover, attaches value to them. But between the two discourses, these words have different meanings; they do not each have a meaning of their own. In the conservative discourse, *liberties*, *rights* and *natural* are all tied to 'inheritance', and *rights* are synonymous with 'privileges'. Through this other and antagonistic construction of meanings, *liberty* could be understood as a 'noble freedom' – 'By this means our liberty becomes a noble freedom' (p. 49). That phrase, indicating the priority of birth and hereditary descent, would have been a contradiction in terms in the liberal bourgeois discourse.

At this stage, it may be useful to review the arguments developed. They go beyond Althusser's statement that, in political, ideological and philosophical struggle, words may be weapons, explosives or tranquillisers and poisons. Occasionally, the whole class struggle may be summed up in the struggle for one word against another word. Certain words struggle amongst themselves as enemies. Other words are the site of an *ambiguity*: the stake in a decisive but undecided battle. (1968a, coll. 1971, p. 24, quoted in Pêcheux 1975, trans. 1982, p. 153)

For they indicate that such struggle over words has to do with how words are put together. It has to do with how, in a 'discursive process', words may be exchanged in full or part for other words (in the example outlined, *natural* for *equal* rights, or *rights* for inherited *privileges*). Pêcheux's theory, which develops from Althusser's (and especially from the essay on the ISAs), explains that it is through the discourses in which words are used that words take up positions in struggle. The positions, by reference to which words in discourse acquire meanings, are in the end antagonistic. They are effects of antagonisms traversing discourse through ideological apparatuses but rooted outside them (1975, trans. 1982, pp. 153–4). In this way, meanings are gained or lost through struggles in which what is at stake is ultimately quite a lot more than either words or discourses.

It seems to me that this suggests how important practical action, rather than intention, is, even in speech or writing. No author and no reader changes the meanings of words. The struggle of discourses changes their meanings, and so the combination in which we put words together matters, and the order of propositions matters: through these, whatever our intentions, words take on meaning. In the example given, this can be seen among a small group of texts. Taking a larger sample, one could study the ways in which words changed their meanings when transposed from orthodox religion to literary criticism in the nineteenth century: the politics of meaning is not confined to the more evidently political discourses. But my account has concentrated specifically on the combination, in antagonistic discourses, of a few words. Even so, like any account, it is not altogether complete; in particular, it does not display the ideological practices with which discourses are linked, nor the institutions to which they are related. Examples of these relations, for a number of discourses, are taken up in chapter 6.

To make quite clear that no individual determines meaning it may be helpful to take an even smaller sample of writing or just one text. An experiment with a single text was undertaken at the Centre National de la Recherche Scientifique (CNRS) in Paris, and recounted in 'Are the Masses an Inanimate Object?' by Pêcheux (1978) as one of the researchers involved. They used a page from the 1972 Mansholt report, and that choice, he recounts, had a certain point to it. The report, by Sicco Mansholt, espoused a theory which advocated radical change and rigorous economic planning as a solution to the crises in capitalist countries. But the theory and the report were reformist and, because of this, ambiguous in their proposals. The experiment focused on this 'ideological ambiguity of reformism' (p. 252).

To generate data, the researchers presented one page from the report to 50 students, young executives on a refresher course. The students 'were not told that the text came from the report':

> Rather, when the first series of 25 students received the text, it was ascribed to a group of left-wing economists. A second series of students received exactly the same text only it was ascribed this time to a completely different source, this time to the right, to a source in the ruling bourgeois government. (pp. 152–3)

They were asked, having read and returned the text, to summarize it in a dozen lines. In this way, the researchers obtained two sets of summaries, which they referred to as the *'left corpus'* and the *'right corpus'* (p. 253).

This assembly of a double corpus was itself a kind of 'political and ideological hypothesis'. It was postulated, in this assembly, that a working out of three ambiguities would result in 'a dissociation of the discursive processes entangled in the Mansholt report' (p. 255). There were the ambiguities inherent in the text, and, secondly, the ambiguity of the ascription of the text. The students involved in the exercise all had similar backgrounds in 'the French intellectual *petite bourgeoisie*' and thus there was also the ambiguous (petite bourgeoisie) class position of the participants (pp. 253, 255). In fact, the working out of these ambiguities, far from creating a general muddle, led to some interesting and precise results.

To analyse the data, the researchers made use of the 'automatic analysis of discourse' which is a partly computerized procedure (p. 254). This was used to display the characteristics both of the Right corpus and of the Left corpus. Although the same words and phrases – *planning, political change, radical reform, government action* – were found to occur in both sets, these words changed their meaning from one corpus to the other. As concerns *planning*,

> the Right corpus focuses the debate on the need for *planning of consumption* . . . insisting on its control and surveillance. The Left corpus on the other hand is oriented to the contrary idea of *centralized planning pertaining to production* . . . implying the need to change economic and political structures. (p. 258)

The same word, *planning*, in expressions summarizing the same original text, was a point of differentiation between two opposing discourses.

In conclusion, we may acknowledge how impossible is a

'universal semantics', a common-sense understanding outside politics and ideology of words, such as *planning*, or of any text. Because the Mansholt report was reformist, the ambiguities of the text were particularly and directly visible. However, it would seem to be the case that any text is, directly or indirectly, a site of some unequal struggle between conflicting discourses and positions. The exercise at the CNRS emphasizes how, in the struggle of discourses, words change their meaning. Here it would be unhelpful to look to persons or things for an explanation. While the changes did not arise out of speaking about different things, neither did they arise subjectively: no person, no individual (Mansholt, the students, or the researchers) could be called the creator of these changes of meaning. That is precisely because 'history, that is to say, the class struggle', which runs through and organizes the relations between discourses, 'is neither a person nor a thing' (pp. 265–6).

There are still one or two problems which need to be sorted out, given that words take on meanings in conflicting discourses and not in a common language. The work done by Pêcheux, from a materialist position, raises and indeed advances the question of 'science', along lines which will be considered in the next section. His work also raises the problem of how language relates to discourses. Many linguists suppose that language is simply an 'instrument of communication'. But such an 'instrument' would be an unlikely basis for conflicting discourses. Here discourse theory can open up a new direction for linguistic research.

Pêcheux proposes that language allows both communication and non-communication, taking his cue from the broad outlines of Renée Balibar's studies of national and fictive French. These he summarizes to show the action of two historical processes: the first coming from within the anti-feudal struggle of the bourgeoisie, and the second from within its struggle against the working class.

Since the Revolution, he suggests, there has been firstly a

move towards uniformity, 'aiming politically and ideologically to set up a national language against the dialects and Latin' so that there might be free communication among everyone. Secondly, through education (for example, through the teaching of grammar as mentioned in chapter 2), there has been a move to impose an 'inegalitarian division'. This move has aimed politically and ideologically to put up '"inside language" class barriers' so that everyone may not have the same access to the language (Pêcheux 1975, trans. 1982, pp. 8–9). He takes this as an instance of how a supposedly common language has been brought to act as an 'instrument' which allows both communication and non-communication (pp. 8–9, 59–60).

From this, he argues that there are, in effect, differences in the access to and handling of the same language by the social classes. Those differences may be imposed through prevailing practices. But thereafter such different usages of the language can be reinscribed in the conflicts of meaning which stem from ruling and ruled ideologies set up antagonistically (pp. 58–60). In this way, discourses may combine imposed differences in the handling of the language with meanings antagonistically constructed. And the effect of this combination is that 'there are contrasting "vocabulary-syntaxes" and "arguments", which lead, *sometimes with the same words*, in different directions depending on the nature of the ideological interests at stake' (p. 9).

To sort out the modes in which languages exist and the relations which they have with discourses, further work – both historical and linguistic – will be required. It appears to be the case that the same language can allow communication and non-communication and be put to use by opposing discourses. In this case, how should one conceive the system of the language? Here Pêcheux's argument raises what seems to me a fundamental issue for linguistic research.

Scientific discourse

The question of 'science' has been left in some suspense while I have drawn on Pêcheux's work to indicate how discourses can find their meanings by reference to ideological positions. This being so, must a special plea be made for discourse in the sciences to rescue it and make it seem separate from ideology? Or must any mention of scientific discourse be dismissed as nonsense on the grounds that 'science' is just the most 'convenient' (i.e. prevailing) ideology of the day?

Pêcheux's concern is with the natural sciences and historical materialism (the Marxist science of history). Working from the propositions that the real is material and only what really exists can be *known*, he takes objectivity as 'scientific' and tends to view 'science' (perhaps simplistically) as the real in the mode in which it must be thought (pp. 140 and 128). Out of the theory he develops, one part seems to me particularly important: a defence of the category of 'science' in relation to the natural sciences and the science of history, or, rather, in relation to their opening up of the continents of material nature and history to exploration.

In fact, in explaining how it makes sense to speak of 'science' and even of 'scientific discourse', Pêcheux's theory marks a step forward. For he avoids the trap into which the questions above would draw one – the rhetorical 'either-or' which insists that either the sciences, in their practice and discourse, are neutral and unpositioned or they are class sciences. Althusser has indicated the dangers of that trap (1974, coll. 1976b, pp. 116–20). The one way returns us to a non-materialist understanding of ideology as illusion, and opposes science to ideology as truth miraculously escaping falsity. The other supposes that science is divided along class lines – bourgeois and proletarian – necessitating its reconstruction after a social revolution. Neither way will do.

Part of Pêcheux's solution – though tempting – is inadequate. He tries to argue that 'the concepts of a science as such do not strictly speaking have a meaning' (1975, trans. 1982, p. 137). But this involves him in making too much of a general distinction between ideologies and sciences, as if the former bring about subjective identifications and the latter do not (pp. 137, 194–5). That schema risks once more upholding an ideal opposition between ideology and science in whose interplay individuals are made subjects and set free. As such, it ignores history. Here I will leave unresolved the issue of whether or not concepts are the same as meanings, or whether there is something in scientific discourse (rather than 'outside', in its real object) escaping an ultimately antagonistic construction. For it is on another front that Pêcheux's theory advances, and does so readily by thinking through the relation between scientific discourse and a materialist position.

His argument is that a science is, in its discourse and its practice, linked to a materialist position, which is on the side of and orientated towards the real. Materialism is no guarantee of science; instead of some guarantee, there is only the necessity that the real object exists, independently and 'before' it is known. Without this necessity, there is no 'science'. So he develops the argument that the emergence of a science is based on the necessity that 'the real object (in the domain of the natural sciences as in that of history) exists independently of the fact that it is or is not known' (p. 49). What he puts forward cannot be used to prove that a given science refers to the real, although it can be used to indicate that a 'science' of anything abstract or subjective is impossible: only what materially exists can be *known*. Along with this, Pêcheux takes it that 'scientific objectivity' is linked to a materialist standpoint. The mode of linking varies: here the history of the sciences is not all the same. None the less, any given science, in its practice and its discourse is realized through a materialist position and is caught up in ideological, philosophical and political struggle (pp. 141, 143).

All this amounts to more than saying there can be no idealist science and no science of what does not exist. It disposes of 'the myth of "scientific neutrality"' (p. 141). Pêcheux's argument comes to this: scientific practice and discourse operates through an ideological (a philosophical) position to designate the real. All science is linked to a materialist position, and (in so far as it is meaningful) scientific discourse finds its meanings by reference to that position. Hence, here as elsewhere in discourse, there is no 'indifference to words' or 'intertranslatability of questions over and above confrontations' (p. 141). The production of scientific knowledges takes place in struggle. It is 'characterised discursively by the taking up of positions *for* certain words', for meanings, for what they designate, '*against* other words, formulations or expressions' that threaten to block the developing science (pp. 153, 138). In its materialism, then, no scientific discourse ever exists in a 'pure' form outside an antagonistic relation to idealist and comparable positions from which it is continuously separating. It never rests secure (pp. 134–43).

From this, he can make clear that 'the history of the production of knowledges is not *above* or *separate from* the history of the class struggle' (p. 134). It is under historical conditions, determined in the last instance by the state of the class struggle, that an emergent science irrupts among the ideologies and is linked to the winning out of materialism over idealism within one domain. A given science breaks with some ideology; but, as Althusser has perhaps emphasized more than Pêcheux, it does not break with 'ideology in general' (1974, coll. 1976b, pp. 119–20).

The sciences are not, however, all the same, and to go further means attending to some differences. Pêcheux points out that, with the natural sciences, the struggle for the production of knowledges, while unfolding among the theoretical ideologies, has most effect upon the development of new technologies and the organization of labour. Its influence upon the practical forms of ruling (bourgeois) ideology is more limited, often causing no direct upsets (1975, trans. 1982, pp. 144–5). The case with the (Marxist) science of history is different. With this science, the materialist position to which it is linked is inseparable from 'the *practical* (political) interests of the Workers' Movement' (p. 147). This science is *directly* linked to politics. In the domain of history, the (materialist) position for science is inseparable from the taking up of a proletarian class position (p. 152) – which is to say that, for history, materialism conflicts with the interests of the bourgeoisie. Pêcheux concludes, 'So there is not and cannot be a "bourgeois science" of history' (p. 147).

Everything Pêcheux has argued leads away from supposing that science could be divided along class lines – bourgeois and proletarian. He maintains that the position for science is always materialist, whether or not for a given domain of scientific knowledge this position connects directly with the interests of a class. At the same time his argument leads away from trying to suppose some difference in mode and form between scientific and other discourses. All discourses are ideo-logically positioned; none are neutral. The difference he locates concerns both the position, which for science is materialist, and the independent or 'prior' existence of the object, in the absence of which there would be no scientific objectivity. In this way, he makes sense of the philosophical category of 'science', showing how that word may be used and defended. And he disarms the attempts of epistemology to guarantee that scientific discourse is '"true" over and above any position taken' (p. 152).

4

Discourse and the critique of epistemology

The sciences can only test their results using their own terms and methods. They do not guarantee that these methods are neutral and true. Such concern with the 'truth' of the sciences is idealist: it belongs to epistemology, the branch of philosophy (ultimately of idealist philosophy) concerned with posing and resolving the problem of how 'valid' knowledge is possible. Setting out from knowledge generally, epistemology tries to prove that there is an overall mode whereby knowledge correlates with reality. It seeks to provide a guarantee that some forms of discourse (but not others) by following the approved mode will give 'valid' knowledge.

There is a range of sciences and of disciplines which are said to give some kind of knowledge (genetics, historical materialism, psychoanalysis, literary criticism, etc.), but they are clearly not all the same. Where they conflict, epistemology can be called in to adjudicate between them, accrediting some and discrediting others. Above all, epistemology functions within bourgeois ideology to impose, even on the material sciences, an appearance of neutrality and truth. In this way, their power or lack of it seems guaranteed, whether by reason or by the way things are; and awkward questions about how the development of knowledges is socially controlled, how knowledges are used, what interests they serve, can all be conveniently forgotten.

Epistemology, according to Althusser, is 'bourgeois ideology's trap of traps. For the simple *question* to which the "theory of knowledge" replies is still a *question of Law*, posed in terms of the validity of knowledge' (1974, coll. 1976b, p. 117). Foucault's work (discussed in chapter 5) covertly dismantles the trap; so will any work on discourse that looks at the social and material existence of knowledges, without regard for their 'truth'. An overt critique of epistemology may look more damaging but is more of a risk.

That risk has been taken by Hindess and Hirst. In a series of books written in the seventies, they call into question the logic (not the rhetoric or the politics) of epistemology. In their critique, rational logic is still accorded the same apparent privilege it has in traditional philosophy. Theirs is an internal critique which, in the act of challenging epistemology, effects a counter-identification with it. Even so, the critique is in many ways helpful, although the uses they make of it, in constructing a theory and an analysis of discourse, are not.

Before moving to Hindess and Hirst's arguments, we may do well to consider the effectivity of critiques, taking Althusser's critique of the 'subject' as an initial example. Humanism supplies the experience of the subject (who is always given prior to social relations) as a source of knowledge and a place from which truth comes. To show up this subject as an imaginary construct is crucial, but cannot usefully be a point of departure for another theory, and Althusser does not make it one. His critique takes issue: it accepts the terms of humanism in order to challenge them. If the 'construction of the subject' is made the basis for a new theory, that theory will have its point of departure decided by humanism. Similarly, the act of criticizing epistemology is necessary, if we are to break the hold of prevailing ideologies, and yet this act cannot be used to start a new theory without reinforcing that hold.

Critiques are useful – and insufficient. To go further it is necessary to start from another position (as much of Althusser's and Pêcheux's work does) and begin from what is normally excluded: contradiction, struggle, the material and social existence of knowledges, discourses and consciousness. Here Marxism is instructive in the way it holds out both a revolutionary theory and practice of disidentification with bourgeois ideology. Althusser demonstrates in 'Reply to John Lewis' that Marxist theory does not begin from a denial of the humanist subject who is supposed responsible for history: 'it is man who makes history' (1973, coll. 1976b, pp. 46–8). It begins from another place, from the primacy of the class struggle over social classes and individuals: 'class struggle is the motor of history' (p. 47). Likewise Marxist theory does not begin from a denial that the truth of knowledges and their relation to things can in general be proved. It begins from another place, from the material and social existence of knowledges.

Now, although it may engage with Marxist work on ideologies, not all work on discourse slots neatly into Marxism. Hirst represents the work of Hindess and himself as supporting all conflicts without priority if, that is, these are reformist (1979, pp. 1–13). But the difficulty, if Marxism and the primacy in the last instance of class struggle are forgotten, is that work on discourse disperses conflicts. This can leave potentially oppositional practices not only at odds with each other but also complicit with what they would oppose. Complicity arises where, through lack of a positive starting-point, either a practice is driven to make use of prevailing values or a critique becomes the basis, as in Hindess and Hirst, for a new theory.

For example, the first of these complicities has affected parts of feminist work on literature. In an essay on 'Sexual/Textual Politics', Toril Moi points out that Anglo-American feminist criticism has indeed been 'strong on challenging the literary institution' and in particular has taken issue with 'the patriarchal literary canon' (1983, p. 1). At the same time, however, this feminist work, in promoting an alternative canon of women's writings, has upheld both the idea of a canon and the dominant practices of reading within education. Humanism (which has always acted to subordinate women) is invited in: we are asked to respect the authority of the text and find our female experience in a literature of our own. Elaine Showalter's criticism is a case in point. As Moi has shown, her 'general appeal to human experience draws her dangerously close to the male, critical hierarchy she seeks to oppose for its patriarchal values' (p. 3). In practice, the struggle against patriarchy cannot be reduced to class struggle. But complicity with what is opposed is the cost of severance: feminist humanism, in spite of its commitment, is finally counter-productive.

The second of these complicities directly affects Hindess and Hirst's theory and analysis of discourse, which is based on their critique of epistemology. Their critique is carried out largely on the terrain of the other, counter-identifying with the keystone of traditional philosophy – the theory of knowledge. Critiques of this kind do work if they remain plainly critical. The reason why they are not enough to break the hold of prevailing ideologies is that they are caught between negativity (rejecting what is dominantly affirmed) and complicity (granting primacy to what they oppose). Hindess and Hirst choose the latter, and the choice is ultimately political. Rejecting epistemology, they base their theory of discourse upon the impossibility of epistemology: the point of departure of their theory is decided precisely by what they have rejected. The result is that Hindess and Hirst, although they claim to be Marxists and have been called post-Althusserians, turn their analysis of discourse specifically against Marxism. At the same time, they advance a criterion of political practice taken directly from traditional theory of knowledge – the necessity of learning from 'experience' (1978, p. 263). These and similar arguments have made some way into several areas of oppositional thought in education, both in social sciences and in arts.

With these cautions, we can now move to Hindess and

Hirst's criticisms of epistemology so as to see how far these are helpful, and irrefutable in their own terms, and yet are limited by the modes of counter-discourse and counter-identification in which they are caught. It will be best to look at the critique first, before considering the problems of their consequent theory of discourse. After this, we can return to Althusser, who begins at another point.

Hindess and Hirst

Since the Renaissance, many theories have tried to assert that there is a neutral and general form under which any knowledge (scientific or other) can correlate with reality. Hindess and Hirst focus broadly on two main kinds of theory: empiricism and rationalism.[1] Empiricist epistemologies hold that all valid knowledge derives ultimately from experience. 'Sense-data, cross-sections of consciousness, the facts of observation' are held to be given to the experience of human subjects (Hindess and Hirst 1977a, p. 10). Knowledge results from the subject working inductively, that is, drawing general inferences from the particulars of experience, so that the nature of things is reproduced in thought. Rationalist epistemologies hold that valid knowledge is effected in a different fashion, through the logical order of conceptual thought. Knowledge is possible because the world is rationally ordered: 'a rationalist epistemology conceives of the world as a rational order in the sense that its parts and the relations between them conform to concepts and the relations between them, the concept giving the essence of the real' (pp. 10–11). Rationalism, we can add, often holds that what is illogical must be false and cannot exist.

Epistemologies may combine elements of empiricism and rationalism (Hindess and Hirst cite Kant's as an example). But all seek to establish some form of overall correspondence or correlation between two general spheres: whether words and things, or knowledge and reality. Hindess and Hirst define epistemology as any theory which 'conceives of the relation between discourse and its objects in terms of both a distinction and a correlation between a realm of discourse on the one hand and a realm of actual or potential objects of discourse on the other' (p. 10).

The logical problem which Hindess and Hirst find in all epistemology runs something like this. An epistemology sets up a fundamental opposition (for example, between theory and fact, or between Man as knowing subject and the object to be known), and it lays down the conditions (perhaps, induction or experience) under which theory can correlate with the facts or the subject can know the object. These conditions will be the conditions of valid knowledge. But the whole endeavour *presupposes* knowledge of what a subject, or an object, or theory or fact is. And it *presupposes* knowledge of the conditions under which they can correlate with each other. What validates, they ask, this 'knowledge' and these categories presupposed in the epistemology (Hindess 1977, pp. 5–6, and Hindess and Hirst 1977a, pp. 13–18)?

Their answer is nothing logically can. This can be explained by examining and developing their examples. Either what is presupposed (Man as knowing subject) is taken to be immune to questioning, an absolute given or one whose existence is grounded in the existence of a divine Subject, beyond knowledge (Hindess and Hirst, 1977a, p. 17). Or the epistemology becomes circular, holding, for example, that it is through experience that we can know that what is given in experience does come from objects. Hindess and Hirst can see no way out of this circle. They argue that it is impossible to demonstrate that some form of discourse (empiricist or rationalist) does the trick except through a form of discourse whose truth is simply assumed (1977a, pp. 13–14, and 1977b, pp. 215–16).

They find that all epistemologies and the methods based on them become caught in this circle. Hindess illustrates the point with reference to J. S. Mill's *A System of Logic*, where the 'laws of nature' are to be known through induction. For Mill, 'induction and the canons of inquiry provide a real knowledge of the world because the world is *really* structured by laws. And how do we know that? By induction' (Hindess 1977, p. 197). These circles are inescapable. Thus Hindess and Hirst reject epistemology, because it is short of logical coherence.

Before studying how the work of Hindess and Hirst develops from here, we should consider the possible disadvantages and advantages of their critique. Epistemology is called upon to guarantee a variety of knowledges and give them an air of 'truth'. It has the purpose of establishing that, under specified conditions, discourse can correlate with reality in ways that are neutral or natural. What Hindess and Hirst's critique uncovers, as John Thompson says, is the fact that 'no special class of statements about how language and reality are linked is itself privileged, immune from revision, hence suitable to serve as the sort of guaranteeing metalanguage epistemology classically has sought' (1981, p. 92). The critique usefully disposes of general guarantees which cannot be set to work if they lack coherence, are unfounded or circular.

Without a set of universal truths or a privileged access to reality, nothing can be proved beyond dispute. Oddly enough, it never could be (the epistemologies conflicted); but this was forgotten as often as it was recognized. The critique leaves us with knowledges whose relations to objects cannot be given some unified and guaranteed form: the form of 'truth'. This is no disadvantage.

But it would be a mistake to say that the critique reduces all knowledges to the level of beliefs, or makes them relative to the objects they work upon or the subjects caught up in them.[2] Indeed, Hindess and Hirst do accept that various disciplines and sciences employ criteria to decide the adequacy of their results: they have their own techniques and tests. However, these criteria are specific to the objectives of particular knowledges (Hirst 1979, p. 21). To see what this might mean, we can consider the discipline of educational psychology, in which intelligence tests are used to establish a scale of different abilities. Such tests are deemed adequate provided they are repeatable, are corrected for cultural and social biases, and conform to a 'normal distribution curve'. These criteria of adequacy are internal to psychology. Hindess and Hirst's critique suggests why there can be no overall guarantee that these criteria are valid or true, no neutral basis for supposing that the differences established belong *naturally* to the children.

This example discloses how getting rid of epistemology can have positive advantages. If epistemological guarantees are worthless, we have no need to evaluate knowledges in terms of any general idea of truth or falsity. We can question knowledges in other ways, as Althusser and Foucault do, questioning their historical conditions, their effects, what interests they serve, what relations of power they uphold.

Hindess and Hirst, however, do not take this step: they see the effects of their critique differently. Instead of leaving epistemology and moving on to other issues, they negate epistemology point by point. For example, theories of knowledge suppose that objects such as steam-engines, phosphorus or capitalist relations of production exist independently of the discourses which describe them. Hindess and Hirst deny this distinction and they hold that objects which discourse refers to cannot exist 'when we do not speak of them' although other unknowable objects can (1977a, p. 20). Fortunately, this is not a necessary consequence of the failing of guarantees. Their critique makes clear that theories of knowledge, being circular and unfounded, are 'logically incoherent' (Hindess 1977, p. 212). But it does not follow that an exact reversal of all epistemological suppositions will be any more coherent.

Hindess and Hirst remain caught in the shadow of

epistemology, and their mistake is to negate its every detail. They systematically eradicate every trace of a distinction and a correlation between discourse and exterior objects. And on the basis of this negation, they construct their theory and analysis of discourse. Besides being unnecessary, this enterprise involves complicity and we may well suspect its politics, for it is directed unswervingly against Marxism. In fact, having shown up epistemology as illusory in its claims, Hindess and Hirst cannot let go of 'bourgeois ideology's trap of traps'. The result is that their theory of discourse is in many ways reactionary and idealist. But because this theory has some currency (especially in social sciences) it is important to see where it leads and where it goes wrong.

Everything is discourse?

On discourse, Hindess and Hirst seem like simple idealists who argue that only ideas exist – except that their theory is more complicated. Although they treat discourses as virtually disembodied, they do allow that no form of discourse (political, theoretical or other) can exist by itself. What seems most simply idealist is their argument that all objects referred to in a discourse (relations of production, neutrons and so forth) exist only in discourse and have no existence outside it. This looks like an assertion that there is nothing outside discourse. But, without an epistemology, they cannot know this, and they are therefore careful to reject any contention that this is so. Their argument is complex, qualified and not always consistent: its effect is, more or less, to take ideas as a starting-point and proclaim their reality: 'ideas are real. . . . they are as real as the economy' (Hirst 1976a, coll. 1979, p. 28). This is, to say the least, a little strange.

It may be questioned what Hindess and Hirst mean by *discourse*. In fact, their definition, far from all-embracing, is limited. 'Discourses' are 'concepts in definite orders of succession, producing definite effects (posing, criticising, solving problems) – as a result of that order' (1977a, p. 7). In other words, they define a discourse as nothing more or less than a sequence of meanings, omitting to consider the technical and institutional processes in which discourses are embodied. Their concern is 'discourse in general' which they gloss as 'speaking and writing' (p. 7). We should notice immediately that their orientation towards a universal form, 'discourse in general', prevents them from attending to the historical conditions and material existence of discourses.

Thus, in analysing a discourse, Hindess and Hirst take account only of the internal sequence of meanings. This distinguishes their work quite sharply from that of Althusser or Pêcheux which is turned towards the contradictory relations between and across apparatuses and practices, in which discourses take shape. Indeed, Hindess and Hirst insist that a 'rigorous separation should be maintained' between questions to do with (a) 'the logical character of the order of concepts of discourse' and (b) 'the process of production or generation of discourse' (Hindness 1977, p. 223). Their analysis is concerned solely with the former.

This method, as Hindess and Hirst recognize, is based on no necessity (1977a, p. 73). The separation they call for assumes that a discourse can be meaningful in itself. Moreover, their method of internal analysis discounts any effects of rhetoric and politics, even effects 'inside' a discourse, in connecting words and propositions: it reduces everything to rational logic and assumes that a discourse simply coheres or fails to cohere through the logical connections between statements. Here it is clear that Hindess and Hirst have returned to the fold (if they ever left it) of traditional idealism. A brief review of alternatives in philosophy will explain this.

Following Althusser, we can say that 'philosophy divides': it is, not immediately but 'in the last instance, class struggle in the field of theory' (1968b, coll. 1971, p. 31, and 1973, coll.

1976b, p. 37). There is a difference, of no small moment and crucial to grasp, between traditional idealism and Marxist or other philosophies of contradiction, and we can put it in this way: idealism gives primacy to the idea or logos; Marxism gives primacy to contradiction and struggle. When it comes to the analysis of discourse, what this difference involves is that traditional analyses look for the logic of the discourse, for its meaning in itself, while Marxist and comparable analyses look for the politics of discourses, for their antagonistic relations. The difference concerns what is to be dominant: if we look for the politics of discourse, we do not evacuate questions of logic and rhetoric. However, in being traditional, Hindess and Hirst do tend to be reductive, reducing everything to rational logic.

They give, and can give, no justification for this. Traditional analyses have been upheld by the epistemological guarantee that what is at stake is an ultimate truth, and that logic provides access to truth. Without this guarantee, the traditional privileging of logic cannot justify itself or claim to be disinterested and above politics. On the other hand, philosophies of contradiction need no guarantee, because they have never claimed to be disinterested (which is why they are gaining ground through the downfall of guarantees).

A few words about Marxist philosophy and science will indicate how Hindess and Hirst's logicized mode of analysis is not disinterested. Marxist philosophy (to simplify) can be exemplified in the thesis cited earlier of the primacy, in the last instance, of class struggle. It is Althusser whose essays since 1968 have remarked again and again that this thesis is a political thesis 'before' it is a philosophical one (and how could it be otherwise?). The correctness (that is, the political correctness and not the truth) of concepts in Marxist science is an effect of this thesis. Marx's *Capital* is, as Althusser points out, the scientific theory of a mode of production (capitalism) based on the exploitation of wage-earning labour power:

If there are workers, that means they are wage-earners and therefore exploited: if there are wage-earners, who own only their labour power which they are obliged (by hunger, says Lenin) to sell, that is because there are capitalists who own the means of production and purchase labour power to exploit it, to extract from it surplus-value. The existence of antagonistic classes is therefore inscribed in production itself, *at the heart of production*: in the relations of production. (Althusser 1971, coll. 1976a, p. 64)

Concepts in Marxism – concepts of class, relations of production, surplus-value, etc. – have a political, before they have a logical, connection with each other. And nothing in Marxist science can be understood unless this little fact is grasped.

Hindess and Hirst do not grasp this little fact. To place their analysis of Marxist discourse, it is enough to notice that they read the thesis of the primacy of class struggle as if it could be first of all philosophical – a thesis called in to guarantee the order of concepts within Marxism (Hindess and Hirst 1977a, pp. 4–5). This makes no sense. Even so, they lose the thesis, taking it as a guarantee, and lose with it all political connections within Marxism. Thus they are left promoting logical coherence in place of politics: promoting, as Anthony Giddens says, 'what is "necessary" to render Marx's discourse internally coherent' (1982, p. 112). Being unable to make it cohere in terms of 'pure' logic, Hindess and Hirst reject Marxism. Their project was directed to this conclusion from the start.

Hindess and Hirst's method of analysis is linked to a theory of discourse. The task of devising a general theory of discourse and its objects, without epistemology, may seem an implausible venture. None the less, this is what they offer: 'We attempt to explain how discourse may be conceived . . . when it is not supposed that it corresponds to or appropriates unities of being external to it in a relation of "knowledge", (1977a, p. 8). The starting-point, then, is a negation of epistemology; and the outcome is a new, and currently fashionable, form of idealism which holds that there is no social whole – everything is dispersed and plural.

What is at stake here is whether discourses can have reference to an outside. Hindess and Hirst deny that they can: whatever things a discourse refers to 'are constituted in it and by it' (1977a, p. 20). Ideas set up things. Negating the epistemological distinction between discourses and outward things, Hindess and Hirst suppose objects of discourse exist only in discourse: 'There is no question here of whether *objects of discourse* exist independently of the discourses which specify them. Objects of discourse do not exist at all in that sense: they are constituted in and through the discourses which refer to them' (1977b, pp. 216–17). Their argument is not a virtual tautology – a mere reminder not to confuse things in a discourse with objects outside it. Its implications are quite other: the objects which a discourse refers to are formed by it and so can only exist through it.

This last is an extreme argument. Let us take an example and see what it means. *Biographia Literaria* (by Coleridge) was published in 1817. Poorly reviewed at the time, it was subsequently valorized as Literature and is now used in education for various purposes. Deconstructionist, Marxist, or liberal humanist studies of literature will probably refer to it in different ways. Now, Hindess and Hirst's argument would deny that the *Biographia* exists outside the various critical discourses through which 'it' is formed and reformed differently. Their argument would require a plurality of different '*Biographias*' with no common properties unless out of chance similarities in the discourses. Aside from this, or from the counter-argument that the *Biographia* has a necessary or natural essence which determines how it is studied and used in education, there are other possibilities. Not least, that the *Biographia* is known differently through different dis-

courses while its social and material existence remains a
precondition of any study that refers to it.

In their theory, Hindess and Hirst tend to assume that
whatever lacks necessity ought to be reversed. 'Reality' has no
necessary essence, so they reverse this and refuse 'common
properties to the referents different discourses constitute'
(Hirst 1979, p. 19). But their reversal does not have to follow;
there are other possibilities. However, to grant that the
referents of different discourses can have common properties
is to allow that a discourse, instead of making what it refers
to, can have reference to what already exists, socially and
materially. And this is part of what Hindess and Hirst wish to
deny.

The outcome of their argument is that monsters are as real
as material things: both come and go in like fashion, according
to the vagaries of discourse (p. 21). 'Reality' is made up of the
referents and constructs of all different discourses. Everything is dispersed and plural: 'One has . . . to accept the
difference of the referents of discourse, the potential infinity
of referents' (p. 19).

What has given the argument credibility is its claim to be
logical, while its supposed continuity with Althusser's
materialist theory of ideology has blurred its idealism. In a
paper of 1976, explaining Althusser's essay on the ISAs, Hirst
attributed to Althusser a curious assertion:

> The second thesis runs as follows: *Ideology is not ideal
> or spiritual.* . . . . Althusser insists that ideology does not
> consist of 'ideas' as opposed to matter. . . . Ideas are not
> to be counterposed to matter or reality. For Althusser,
> ideas are real and not 'ideal' because they are always
> inscribed in social practices and expressed in objective
> social forms (languages, rituals, etc.). . . . . Ideologies are
> social relations, they are as real as the economy. (Hirst
> 1976a, coll. 1979, pp. 27–8)

'Ideas are real.' There is only one difficulty with viewing this statement as materialist – how to make sense of it without following the idealist route, marked out by Hindess and Hirst, to the point where ideas set up things. But, in fact, the ISAs essay reads differently; Hirst has substituted mere negations for its positive proposals. Althusser's second thesis runs as follows: 'Ideology has a material existence' (Althusser 1970, coll. 1971, p. 155). What this means is that 'ideas' and 'representations' are neither ideal nor real, for they have no existence of their own: an 'ideology always exists in an apparatus, and its practice, or practices. This existence is material' (p. 156). Ideologies take shape in apparatuses, in their practices, and exist antagonistically through the relations between the 'classes at grips in the class struggle' (pp. 142, 173). Not ideas, then, but their modes of existence are real. From this, we can see that in no sense do Hindess and Hirst follow Althusser.

But there are other problems with the contention that a discourse does not refer outside itself, that what it refers to is 'constituted in it and by it' (Hindess and Hirst 1977a, p. 20). Given this argument, it is not surprising that Hirst's explanation turns Althusser's theory of ideology into non-sense, nor that Hindess and Hirst lose the political connections in Marxist discourse. What they have to say about discourses generally, or about Marx's *Capital* or about Althusser's theory of ideology concerns only objects formed within their discourse.[3] To allow otherwise is to allow that discourses, instead of making what is referred to, can refer to what already exists. In the end, their theory is as useful as *Monopoly* – and the rules are more complicated.

Finding that epistemology is 'logically incoherent' (Hindess 1977, p. 212), and at the same time holding onto the possibility of a 'pure' logic, Hindess and Hirst set up a theory of discourse through negating epistemology. But their theory is no more coherent. To avoid their conception of discourse, and not encounter the difficulties of Hindess and Hirst's begin elsewhere, as Althusser does.

The politics of philosophy

Althusser's recent theory (since 1968) affords us a way of escaping the epistemological circle, without letting go of knowledge or of reference to real objects. To understand how it is possible to accept the lack of epistemological guarantees and not encounter the difficulties of Hindess and Hirst's project, we need to make what may seem a detour and consider philosophy itself a little further, in its categories and in its politics.

Now, although Hindess and Hirst turn Althusser's materialism upside down, there is one point of agreement: philosophical discourse. Althusser has argued that 'philosophy has no object', and that it is not a knowledge, least of all is it 'Absolute Knowledge' (1973, coll. 1976b, pp. 68, 58). But, from a materialist standpoint, this deficit applies specifically to philosophy; it does not concern the sciences. We can explain this argument by saying that philosophy is theory of the general and universal (ideology in general, discourse in general, etc.), and so cannot be a knowledge of objects which have a historical and material existence. However, this does not mean that philosophy is 'pure contemplation, pure *disinterested* speculation' (p. 57). On the contrary, no philosophy is neutral. Even a philosophy that seeks to refuse priorities and to undo distinctions, if it retains any meaning, is not neutral—its standpoint is implied both in its assumptions and its refusals and also in the methods it deploys.

Tendencies in philosophy, Althusser has argued, 'group themselves in the last instance around the antagonism between idealism and materialism' (1974, coll. 1976b, p. 142). We can grasp philosophy as a field of conflict in which a thesis, or proposition, is defined through its antagonism to other theses. Within this field, he suggests, there can be no purely materialist, or purely idealist philosophy given as a simple presence, 'because a philosophy only exists in so far as it "works out" its difference from other philosophies' (p. 133).

But all positions in philosophy have political effects. This is part of what Althusser indicates by saying that 'philosophy is, in the last instance, class struggle in the field of theory' (1973, coll. 1976b, p. 37). In refusing the priority of what is referred to in *any* discourse, whether philosophical or scientific, Hindess and Hirst give primacy to discourse itself and locate 'objects' within it. Such a theory has political consequences, not least in that, by dispersing discourses and the struggles which act through them, it seeks to discount all attempts to change the social whole; it is an idealist philosophy with consequent effects for politics. Idealist philosophies advantage only those who have an interest in profiting from the existing state of affairs.

Like Hindess and Hirst, Althusser criticizes epistemology. But the position from which he does so is different, and his critique concerns in the end the politics more than the logical incoherence of epistemology. From Descartes to Kant, the dominant philosophy has brought both humanism (theory of the subject as origin) and empiricism (theory of experience) under idealism. This tradition, Althusser argues, has privileged the 'category of the "Subject" as Origin, Essence and Cause, *responsible* in its internality for all the determinations of the external "Object"' (p. 96). In other words, this tradition has promoted Man, in his ideas and experience, as the source of knowledge, morals and history. To criticize any part of this tradition from within in an act of counter-identification serves ultimately to perpetuate it. Althusser starts from elsewhere, from materialism. And it is from a materialist position, in an act of disidentification, that he has come, since 1968, to give up any project for a general theory of knowledge – because of 'the idealism or idealist connotations of all Epistemology' (1974, coll. 1976b, p. 124).

His argument calls for brief explanation. Epistemology, in its search for guarantees, has been primarily concerned with the 'problem' of how the subject can have knowledge of the object. The problem is idealist in that it supposes a subject or spiritual consciousness as the origin and justification of knowledge. Even if we suppose that the object is the origin of knowledge, we have not escaped idealism – for the object can only be the origin if the idea already exists in it as its essence. Finally, any search for general guarantees supposes that knowledge has a universal and ideal form; it 'forgets' that procedures of knowledge change and come about under specific material and historical conditions. Outside idealism, 'every question of the Origin, Subject and Justification of knowledge, which lie at the root of all theories of knowledge, is rejected' (1975, coll. 1976b, p. 188).

Awareness of the idealism of epistemology will not require us to treat its categories as pure ideas. Althusser displays them as legal metaphors, and suggests that the problem of knowledge has been set up by 'the presence of Law and of legal ideology' in bourgeois philosophy (1974, coll. 1976b, p. 117). The category of the 'subject' responsible for knowledge is a legal category; and the antithesis between subject and object (or person and thing) is a basic part of capitalist law. More than that, the function of any epistemological criterion of truth is legalistic: 'for it only represents a form of Jurisdiction, a Judge to authenticate and guarantee the validity of what is True' (p. 137). Althusser (following Spinoza in this) refuses any epistemological guarantee or criterion of truth, as do Hindess and Hirst. But the mode in which he does so differs notably from theirs. By relinquishing epistemology because of its idealism, he brings about the advantages of their critique – without the disadvantages. As the outcome of a standpoint fully antagonistic to idealism, this relinquishing cannot provide occasion for a general theory of discourse and its objects (such as Hindess and Hirst supply) or for supposing that knowledges and sciences refer to no real objects.

There is in the sciences no ultimate neutrality. Arguing this, Althusser can still consider that they are knowledges of what exists. Letting go of epistemology does not lead him to deny knowledge or prevent him talking about it. This is because his rejection of epistemology is made from a materialist position and the very basis of materialism is the thesis of 'the primacy of being over thought'. This thesis says several things at once; let me take just one of them: the real object exists independently of how it is known, and as a precondition for any knowledge of it – 'only what exists *can be known*' (1973, coll. 1976b, pp. 54–6). In other words, scientific knowledge can come about only where the object really exists (1975, coll. 1976b, pp. 190–1). Bourgeois philosophy would at once step in and ask, 'how do you know? where is the guarantee, the philosophical proof?' There is only one reply: philosophy is not a knowledge and there are no guarantees.

Philosophy is neither objective nor verifiable. Its theses, as we have seen, can neither have nor act as guarantees. Philosophy is not thereby a nullity. Philosophical theses, materialist or idealist, have political as well as theoretical effects and, as Althusser points out, they have these effects in the sciences and in other social practices.

The thesis of the primacy of being over thought draws a line of demarcation. It is a position which reminds us that in disputes over knowledge (for example, knowledge of history) something real is at stake. And this is crucial to avoid two current tendencies in philosophy, both of which open a space for propagandist fictions and cannot oppose even outright inventions of 'events' and 'objects'. The one tendency ('forgetting' politics) can deny or pacify disputes in the name of the '*difference* of the referents of discourse', to quote once more from Hirst (1979, p. 19). The other tendency is reductive, asserting that disputes over knowledge, conflicts between discourses, are *only* political disputes.

Althusser points out that the thesis of the primacy of being over thought, to be properly materialist, must imply a distinction between the real object and the object of knowledge. 'Thought' does not exist in the real object nor does the real object exist 'in thought' (1975, coll. 1976b, pp. 190–2). How, then, does 'thought' refer to the real object? We should notice, immediately, that Althusser does not ask this question. For the 'thought' he is discussing 'is not . . . absolute consciousness confronted by the real world as matter' (1968, trans. 1970, p. 41). 'Thought' is his philosophical shorthand for existing discourses, meanings and knowledges which take shape under specific material and historical conditions (p. 41). To ask how 'thought' refers to the real is to suppose a general process of knowledge unifying, for example, physics and the Marxist science of history. The materialist response is to find the question inappropriate because the sciences have different procedures and practices of reference, and the objects they refer to have different modes of materiality: nature and history are not the same.

The thesis of the primacy of being over thought does not, therefore, lead to an epistemology; it leads away from one. To see its positive effects in philosophy and in knowledges, we can take the example of Marxist theory, on which Althusser focuses. Marxist theory, he emphasizes, contains both a science, the science of history or historical materialism, and a philosophy, dialectical materialism. Within the philosophy, the thesis of the primacy of being specifies, for history, the economy (the material base) as the ultimately determining element. Althusser cites Engels: 'According to the materialist conception of history, the *ultimately* determining element in history is the production and reproduction of real life' (1975, coll. 1976b, p. 176). He is careful to point out that the economy is not to be thought of as the centre or unitary origin of the social whole (that way lies an idealist philosophy of the Origin). The economy determines, in the last instance, a social whole which is complex and uneven – because the economy is itself uneven, a site of contradiction and struggle (pp. 181–5). Under capitalism, the primary economic contradiction is between labour and capital, a contradiction which sets up class struggle between the proletariat and the bourgeoisie (1973, coll. 1976b, p. 50). The primacy of being, of the economy, and of class struggle are, then, interconnected propositions. Philosophical theses have links connecting them.

When it comes to scientific knowledges, philosophy has effects that are at once political and theoretical. To understand these effects, we cannot simply assume that philosophy is applied to problems in the sciences. Althusser argues that 'philosophy cannot be applied', and this makes sense because general propositions can, as we have seen, give no knowledge. Philosophy works instead in a different way 'by modifying the *position* of the problems' (p. 58). In other words, theses orient the knowledge and its discourse, methods, investigations.

The crucial importance of materialist theses is that these orient the investigator towards the objectivity and modes of material existence of what is being investigated. Materialism, in the study of history, will not make us suppose that capitalism either has some necessary existence or is constituted by discourse. Instead, materialism will point to the historical emergence and the material and social existence of capitalism. To take a very different example, when we are studying literature, materialism will not have us suppose that literature is the outcome of Man's creative spirit. Instead, it will show up the apparatuses and practices, and their discourses, through which certain writings have been and are valorized as literature. Any knowledge of what exists materially and historically is a knowledge of what can be changed. It is not a neutral knowledge – no knowledge is.

Now, if we follow this orientation in investigating knowledges and discourses themselves, finally we have a way of leaving epistemology far behind. For this orientation leads to the study of 'the material, social, political, ideological and philosophical conditions . . . of already existing knowledge' (Althusser 1974, coll. 1976b, p. 124). The study which Althusser outlines is still very much in its infancy. To begin, it has had to break and must go on breaking with the preconceptions of the traditional history of ideas. Foucault's investigations of discourse and knowledge, without being fully materialist, are more than a guide here. His work, as we shall see, crucially highlights and dismantles traditional preconceptions – in ways which may well be devastating for them.

5

Foucault's archaeologies of knowledge

Outside the circles of ideal truth, with little wish to write or unwrite guarantees of truth, the 'archaeologist' of knowledge is one who asks what has made possible different knowledges. In the eighteenth century, one could know about madness and folly; today one can know about mental illness. At one time, it was possible to consider language as a means of naming things, and to enquire into the dormant names which composed words of several syllables; later, one could investigate the phonetic sounds. Through a number of studies in the sixties, Foucault developed an 'archaeology' that questioned some of these shifts in western thought over the last 400 years. His studies undertook to lay out some of the historical transformations which, in one way or another, have been 'necessary and sufficient for people to use these words rather than those, a particular type of discourse rather than some other type', or 'for people to be able to look at things from such and such an angle and not some other one' (Foucault 1977e, coll. 1980a, p. 211).

Even since the Renaissance knowledges have changed considerably. More than 200 years ago, there was little trace of those domains which, from psychiatry to literary criticism, now revolve around the figure of man. It was in taking issue with these humanist domains that Foucault's 'archaeology' developed, and its methods deal specifically with them, rather than with the material sciences. This specificity is not in itself a limitation. What does set limits to his archaeologies is that they were written before, at a tangent to, the breakthrough made by the ISAs essay in the study of how meanings are materially constructed. That is to say, they have no sense of the antagonism of discourses, no sense of the struggle for and between knowledges. What makes them of considerable importance, on the other hand, is their critical operation: in particular, they work to dismantle the universal and evident themes of what passes for the history of ideas. In fabricating around knowledges a story of the experience shared in each age, the progressive unfolding of men's thoughts, and their monotonous discoveries of the truth of things, the history of ideas for too long had obstructed other work. Foucault's projects of the sixties were set against it, and in *The Archaeology of Knowledge* (1969, trans. 1972) he identified their critical operation: 'archaeological description is precisely such an abandonment of the history of ideas, a systematic rejection of its postulates and procedures, an attempt to practise a quite different history of what men have said' (p. 138). A major task, not a simple one, was to clear away the themes of continuity, expression and reflection, all of which are ultimately idealist themes.

First of all in this chapter, I will indicate how Foucault's early writings can be seen to track down and dismantle themes in the history of ideas which block materialist work. Besides giving us a critical line, his projects also make new proposals. But these, I wish to suggest, are mainly useful for the difficulties they encounter because of their failure to grasp principles of antagonism and struggle. Here there is little to gain from a fully unified survey of Foucault's work in the sixties, a survey which places the writing under the control of whatever is taken to be the author's final meaning. Authorism of this kind is idealist, and to cover the early writings with a fictitious coherence, fabricating from some end their total sense, would be rather an ironic gesture. Even so, authorship is not just an illusion. Foucault's writings circulate under his name; they are authorized. Because of this, I will take notice of the range of their arguments, and not only of those which are most helpful. To ignore their circulation, to discount its effects, would be a mistake.

Dismantling the history of ideas

To write the history of ideas and treatments of madness is, of course, simple. One need do no more than tell the happy story of how past thoughts and discoveries have made their way, slowly and with some regrettable errors towards the present truths of psychiatry. For mental illness, so the story goes, has an essential nature which knowledge reflects and present knowledge reflects most of all – psychiatry is indeed to be congratulated on its achievements. But there is one small problem with this account. It traces a pure circle from the present to the past to the present, as if nothing ever really changes. In *Madness and Civilization* (1961, trans. 1967), Foucault's rather different study of the history of madness offers a quite remarkable refusal of this idealist theme.[1] The ready-made continuities of the official story are rejected, along with any idea that knowledge is a reflection of the essence of things.

As a first move, his study marks out a discontinuity by referring back before the birth of the asylum and psychiatry to the classical age of the seventeenth and eighteenth centuries. Here it considers 1656, and the royal decree which founded the Hôpital Général in Paris, a 'landmark': the beginning of the great confinement that for a century and a half not only in France but across Europe was to 'assign the same homeland to the poor, to the unemployed, to prisoners, and to the insane' (p. 39). His account, then, does not start from the nature of mental illness and ask how well this was reflected in classical thought. It starts from the institutions which shut up the mad and gave them much the same status as those waylaid by some form of 'unreason', such as 'the debauched, spendthrift fathers', and all those lacking work (p. 65). From this, it arrives at the general meanings attached to all those who were confined. For his study describes how the places of confinement, in their insistence upon work, were a means of punishing idleness and of giving value to an 'ethical consciousness of labour' (p. 55). It was with the meaning of 'social uselessness' that madness was shut up in them (p. 58). He also indicates how, within the places of confinement, specific practices could attach further ideological meanings to madness: put on display, the mad could be exhibited as 'monsters'; in chains and behind bars, they could be seen as 'beasts' and 'animals' (pp. 70–2).

In this way, by starting from institutional confinement in the classical age, Foucault's 'history of madness' dispels the notion that confinement and the psychiatric asylum reflect some eternal truth about human kind. Confinement shut up much more than the asylum has ever laid claim to, and the meanings which were attached there to the mad are, from the point of view of psychiatry, very strange. Foucault's study then turns to 'classical thought'. It details how, in classical thought, just as much as in the practices of confinement, madness was acknowledged as a kind of 'non-being' or 'nothingness' (pp. 115–16). Madness was less a disease of reasoning than an emptiness brought about by dazzlement: it was 'reason dazzled' (p. 108). His argument is that a classical experience of madness 'crops up with the same meanings, in the identical order of its inner logic, in both the order of speculation and the order of institutions, in both discourse and decree, in both word and watchword' (p. 116). What Foucault here called 'the order of institutions' and 'the order of speculation' can be specified, using the concepts of historical materialism, as *practical ideology* and *theoretical ideology*. In the next chapter, I will come back to these. For the moment, it is enough to notice that a history which moves from the one to the other can dismantle the notion that knowledge arises out of things and reflects their essential truth: it leaves no hold for this theme of reflection.

The 'obvious' response is to turn from things to the consciousness of men. The history of ideas depends upon the idealist theme of expression which supposes that men and their ideas have given birth to what is known. Again, 'archaeology' takes apart this theme; Foucault's study of clinical medicine, *The Birth of the Clinic* (1963, trans. 1973), gives us a remarkable dismantling of it. In the process, his archaeology is slightly altered. Concentrating on France, he examines the decades before, during and after the upheavals of the French Revolution. And in that transition, he details certain diverse (economic, political, legal and ideological) conditions out of which the clinic, along with a new domain of knowledge, clinical medicine, was born. His argument is that 'Medicine made its appearance as a clinical science in conditions which define, together with its historical possibility, the domain of its experience and the structure of its rationality' (p. xv). Starting with these conditions, his study avoids the notion that clinical medicine originated in the ideas of doctors. But it does more than this. Resisting the assumption that a medical consciousness was already there influencing the clinical field, it indicates how a new medical consciousness was formed and took shape along with the clinic. In this way, Foucault's study begins the immense task of dismantling the theme that knowledge is an expression of men's ideas.

In its dependence upon themes of expression, the history of ideas slides into both humanism and idealism. It supposes that there is a subject *of* history who, while also a subject *in* history, is the director of events in the theatre in which he finds himself. This subject is always male: his name is Man. To enshrine this little man-god, the history of ideas fabricates its essential continuities: 'Continuous history is the indispensible correlative of the founding function of the subject: the guarantee that everything that has eluded him may be restored to him' (Foucault 1969, trans. 1972, p. 12). Against continuity, Foucault's archaeologies tend to juxtapose different historical moments and in this way mark out breaks in knowledge.

Juxtaposition is not sufficient, however, and in his next project, *The Order of Things* (1966, trans. 1970), Foucault makes a further move to disperse continuities. But the move made constitutes a retreat on the part of archaeology, for it tends to isolate knowledges from other social practices. *The Order of Things* confronts some of the recent disciplines centred on man: psychology, sociology and the analysis of literature and myth (pp. 357–8). Its archaeology suggests that the figure of man on which they focus 'is an invention of recent date. And one perhaps nearing its end' (p. 387). Foucault approaches these humanist disciplines from some distance: he takes three kinds of knowledge from the seventeenth and eighteenth centuries – natural history, analysis of wealth and general grammar – each of which gave way at the end of the eighteenth century to what he calls the sciences of life, labour and language. His study is an attempt to describe part of the arrangement of classical thought and, in contrast to this, the modern arrangement and the particular configuration of modern knowledges which has enabled the disciplines of psychology, etc., and their figure of man to develop. Between the classical and the modern, he locates a rupture which caused the ground of classical thought to crumble: a rift 'that divides in depth the *episteme* of the Western world' (p: 250).

The new notion here, the 'episteme', may be understood as the 'ground of thought' on which at a particular time some statements – and not others – will count as knowledge. Foucault's study posits that knowledges in their very concepts are informed by definite rules; there is a regularity in their development, even though their practitioners are not conscious of these rules. So, in *The Archaeology of Know-*

ledge, the episteme is defined as the *ensemble* of 'relations that can be discovered, for a given period, between the sciences', and the network of connections that can be found between knowledges, 'when one analyses them at the level of discursive regularities' (1969, trans. 1972, p. 191). It is a notion that tends, as Lecourt has said, to suggest that knowledges exist in 'great layers obedient to specific structural laws' (1972, trans. 1975, p. 189). In other words, the notion of the episteme is rather too general, as is the rupture, or rift, described in *The Order of Things*. But its real problem is that it loses the links between knowledges (of whatever kind: whether theoretical ideologies or the sciences that irrupt among them) and other social practices.

Fortunately, there is another way of avoiding the continuities and the 'total history' implicit in the history of ideas. This other way is, in fact, referred to in *The Archaeology of Knowledge* as the materialist 'decentring' (1969, trans. 1972, pp. 12–13). Because it places class struggle in the front rank, materialist history is quite unable to reduce all thought to a single form, to trace a simple continuity in its development, or to give a centre to all knowledge. A materialist history of 'madness' would study, as does Foucault's archaeology, the connection between confinement and classical knowledge of madness. For clinical medicine, it too would detail the various economic and social conditions in which the clinic emerged. But it would do more. Placing class struggle in the front rank, it would set out the politics of knowledge and study how knowledges, in their relations to each other at a given moment, in their links with institutions and in their historical conditions, in the last instance have been informed by class struggles. So it would study the struggles for and between knowledges.

The history of existing knowledges still needs to be written.[2] Foucault's archaeologies begin to clear a space for it: they move to dismantle those idealist notions that all knowledge has a continuous form expressing men's thoughts and reflecting the truth of things. This is their key use. What I wish now to suggest is that archaeology both advances towards the conditions of existing knowledges and stumbles on a series of blocks. Why? Because it is made up principally of counter-discourse: it is a reversal of, rather than a radical departure from idealist themes.

Conditions of knowledge

What is most positive in *Madness and Civilization* is the focus on the connections between knowledges and institutions. Foucault's analysis tends to suggest that the birth of the asylum, at the end of the eighteenth century, made psychiatry possible. Indeed, from his study one might say that asylum practices, in a certain way, assigned the forms and limits of psychiatric knowledge. However, there are also some gaps or, rather, lapses in the analysis.

To demonstrate the conditions which made it possible for psychiatry to appear, Foucault's study describes first of all the break-up of generalized confinement towards the end of the eighteenth century. This disintegration had several determinants. First, there was resistance among those confined to mingling with the mad (1961, trans. 1967, p. 224). Second, with the growth of industry, the poor were increasingly required for the labour force (p. 232). Third, the bourgeois laws, passed during the Revolution in France, ensured that confinement was kept only for 'criminals and for madmen', while proposing separate sites for these (pp. 236–7). His analysis sets the birth of the asylum in this break-up of confinement—as if a space had been created in which the asylum could appear. It then turns to examine practices within the asylum. It takes two instances – the reforming of Bicêtre by Pinel into an asylum for the insane and the setting up by Tuke of an English Quaker asylum, the Retreat – and describes how, in both, asylum life was modelled on forms of bourgeois ideology. For example, in Tuke's Retreat, the mad were treated as children; they were placed under 'family tutelage' in a model of family relations that was both 'bourgeois' and 'patriarchal'. The mad 'child' in the Retreat was submitted to the authority of the Father and to the care of the rational adult – the adult which the child was called to become (pp. 252–3).

Where the Retreat privileged the family, Pinel's asylum was much more juridical. In each case, what Foucault's study suggests is the importance of their institutional 'structures' to the ways in which psychiatry (and later, rather differently, psychoanalysis) took shape. His argument is that the 'structures' in the asylum set up not 'science, but a personality': they set up the physician in full authority as 'Father and Judge, Family and Law' (pp. 271–2). Resting on that personal authority, psychiatry would become in the nineteenth century 'a medicine of a particular style' (p. 275). Psychiatry brought into play 'moral powers' whose roots in the practical structures of the asylum were increasingly lost from sight as the century went on (p. 275). Later, psychoanalysis 'demystified' much of this, and yet exploited to the full the authority of the doctor and prepared 'for its omnipotence a quasi-divine status' which remains the key to psychoanalysis (p. 277).

The importance of this study, in *Madness and Civilization*, lies in its suggestion that institutional practices have a primacy over forms of knowledge. It marks out a shift from confinement to the asylum which was not the effect of new knowledge. Indeed, it suggests that asylum 'structures' gave the shape in which psychiatry was to appear and from which even psychoanalysis would borrow mysteries.

Its difficulty lies in the way it marks out the birth of the asylum. Whereas the break-up of confinement is carefully grasped as an effect of resistance, of bourgeois class struggle and of the requirements of capitalist industry, an attempt is made to situate the new asylum outside any struggle or antagonistic relation. This is, no doubt, the obvious line to take: the old order is ended through conflict; the new is born out of itself in single wonder. But the effect of taking this line is that the study slips back into idealist themes, which in other respects have been so remarkably suspended, when it describes how the asylum found its practices in the new order. It describes the asylum simply as reflecting forms of bourgeois ideology instituted elsewhere: the family structures of Tuke's Retreat are said to be 'a kind of microcosm' imaging in small-scale the 'bourgeois family' (pp. 274, 253). One institution could correspond so simply to others only if there were a subject directing history.

This is not the only way in which Foucault's account slips back into the assumptions it challenges. His study of the earlier practices of confinement and of discourse on madness in the classical age indicates that these were connected. But in explaining how they were connected, it falls back on a notion of 'experience'. It makes much of 'a social sensibility, common to European culture', 'the classical experience of unreason' (pp. 45, 197). This notion of something like a 'world-view', an experience common to all in the age, again assumes that there is a single force, a subject, directing history:

> Generally speaking, *Madness and Civilization* paid for too much attention, in a rather enigmatic way, to what was defined as an experience ['*expérience*'], showing up how close I still was to accepting an anonymous and general subject of history. (Foucault 1969, pp. 26–7)

So *Madness and Civilization*, because it does not take up a sufficient distance, lapses back into some of the very arguments it rejects. Even so, the study, especially of the asylum and psychiatry, gives us on the way an immensely important suggestion that institutional practices have a primacy over forms of knowledge.

Psychiatric knowledge is very 'dubious' and easily upset

(Foucault 1977b, coll. 1980a, p. 109). Clinical medicine is much more solid, and is not unsettled by archaeological excavation. Foucault's archaeology – of the transformation of medicine in the years before, during and after the Revolution in France – does not damage what medicine can do, neither does it favour one kind of medicine over another. What it does again attempt is a study, not shot through with idealist themes, of the conditions of a knowledge – and it makes a move to avoid lapsing back: it attends to the conflicts, particularly in ideology.

His study takes most notice of the political ideology of the bourgeoisie, in which privilege was opposed by liberty. At the start of the French Revolution, the liberal actions to end closed professions, to remove hospitals and the university authorities, and to return the sick to the family as the 'natural' place for them, all seemed to fit in with the way medical knowledge was developing (Foucault 1963, trans. 1973, pp. 38–9). But, at the same time, liberalism, in aiming to abolish the hospitals, 'prevented the organization of clinical medicine' (p. 52). It was in the war years, as quackery became rife, that the call for 'control and supervision' of training made a come-back, and there was a hasty recourse to the hospital not in its old form but as a teaching institution, the clinic (pp. 66–9). His argument is that the clinic came about in neither 'reaction' nor 'progress': 'what occurred was the restructuring, in a precise historical context, of the theme of "medicine in liberty"' (p. 69). This argument suggests that the clinic was born out of conflicting requirements to do with liberty and control. In the case of the clinic, these conflicts seem to have brought about reform. For other institutions and knowledges, in other conflicts, the effect may be quite different.

The attention to conflict is a crucial move. However, this analysis is not sustained in *The Birth of the Clinic*, with the result that the study of clinical medicine also lapses into rejected themes. What Foucault argues is that the clinic 'faltered' for a while because of a 'central lacuna': before the clinic could be set up, there had to be a reorganization of medical thought (p. 51). His study is much concerned with changes in the 'medical gaze', that is, in what doctors could see and say. Using new 'codes of knowledge', doctors were able to see the disease in its symptoms and calculate the outcome (p. 90). Through their gaze, a knowledge could be opened up that was present for all to see, so that the clinic could become a teaching institution in which the medical field was 'no longer divided between those who know and those who do not' (p. 110). The old privileged hold on knowledge, the former distances of the lecture-halls, would be removed in the clinic. Now, this argument makes a serious mistake. It gives primacy to forms of knowledge over institutional practices. Specifically, it supposes that the transformation of the 'gaze' was a centre holding other changes in place: as Foucault later pointed out, 'In this respect, the term "*regard* médical" . . . was not a very happy one' (1969, trans. 1972, p. 54).

What is most important, then, in *The Birth of the Clinic* is the attention though limited to struggle, and in *Madness and Civilization* the grasp of a primacy of institutions over knowledges. But Foucault's archaeologies in the early sixties cannot hold these moves together. This is because both studies are controlled principally by counter-discourse, and so are limited by and remain too near to what they reject. Hence they stumble on a series of blocks (which the notion of the episteme in *The Order of Things* does not remove). Let me risk stating what would remove these blocks: a stronger sense of the struggles for and between knowledges, struggles which are rooted ultimately in real, material relations.

Foucault's studies in the early seventies are not the same: they have much more to tell us. I will come to them in the next chapter. But, first, *The Archaeology of Knowledge* is both a self-review and a new departure. What is most different in it is an argument that the mode in which discourses exist in not just institutional, as Foucault's preceding studies suggest: it is specifically material. This argument – even though it gets tipped upside down, for there is a split running through all the pages of the *Archaeology* – is the index of a key advance.

Problems and advances

There is an excellent article by Lecourt which both criticizes the *Archaeology* and suggests how we may read it. Its descriptions of discourse (that is, of serious discourses or knowledges) are haunted, he contends, by a decisive question: 'the necessity, which Foucault recognizes, to define "the regime of materiality" of what he calls discourse' (Lecourt 1972, trans. 1975, p. 194). Parts of the *Archaeology* have a remarkable consonance with the theory of discourse put forward in chapter 3, although they attend less to how words change their meanings than to how statements have an identity.

In the *Archaeology*, the statement is taken as the 'elementary unit of discourse', and it is argued that any statement 'must have a material existence' (Foucault 1969, trans. 1972, pp. 80, 100). The form in which Foucault spells this out may look superficial at first: 'a statement must have a substance, a support, a place, and a date' (p. 101). However, his explanation extends further and, in so doing, leaves us with no suspicion that material existence might be incidental to the statement, while the subjective intention of the speaker (what he or she has in mind) might be what truly counts. No. Material existence is 'constitutive' of the statement and constructs its identity: the identity of a statement 'varies with a complex set of material institutions' (p. 103). (Such an argument has been fully developed in chapter 3.)

But the ways in which institutions are material are perhaps not made clear in the *Archaeology*. Certainly, it is not merely the case that they are things, composed of fragments of 'matter' (p. 103). From a materialist standpoint, we may say that the mode of materiality of institutions is physical but also social and, as such, is shaped by contradictions rooted, in the last instance, in the real relations of the economy. Foucault's line in the *Archaeology*, which leaves aside these contradictions, is more simplistic: institutions and economic processes are grouped together as what, being 'non-discursive', must be material and can give existence to discourses. That argument is not particularly adequate. But it is enough to suggest that discourses are in some way based in social processes, and it draws a distinction between the kinds of connections which belong to discourse and other 'non-discursive' connections which are '*real* or *primary*' (p. 45). So it gives first place to connections which, 'independently of all discourse or all object of discourse, may be described between institutions, techniques, social forms, etc.'; they are 'primary' (p. 45). This is really quite important, for no other order, no order which took discourses themselves as a starting-point, could even begin to indicate how discourses exist materially.

There are, however, other and grander strains of argument in the *Archaeology* and these tend to pull the text once more in an opposing direction. They home in upon a category which has its first display here, a new invention which looks useful but quickly falls apart: the category of 'discursive practice'. Unlike Foucault's preceding studies, the *Archaeology* describes discourses generally. By using examples from the same sort of fields, it makes some corrections. But the attempt to take discourses as practices can only disorientate the preceding studies; so I will comment no more than briefly on its effects, and then leave it behind. That new category is put together in the *Archaeology* to answer the question of how any one discourse may be identified. Foucault's argument is that a discourse may be identified by a set of rules; and it is these rules which he calls here, in a very curious usage, a 'practice'. They systematically form for the discourse 'groups of objects, enunciations, concepts, or theoretical choices' (p. 181). One of his examples is of rules which form modes of speaking, or 'enunciations', in clinical medicine. They do so by deciding who 'is accorded the right' and the 'status' to make medical statements, and from what 'institutional sites', such as the hospital and the laboratory, statements may come (pp. 50–1).

In this instance, we might suppose that the 'rules' deciding right, status, etc., are somehow set up by social processes outside clinical discourse, though Foucault's proposals cannot tell us how this is. But here the difference in his arguments is revealed. They take the line that such rules 'reside in discourse itself' (p. 74). So, if psychiatry can be a knowledge of delinquency and criminal behaviour, this is not, in the *Archaeology*, held to be because of the way in which psychiatry has been socially constructed in what is in the end a class politics. The line taken, on the contrary, is that it is because a set of rules, a 'group of particular relations', has been 'adopted for use in psychiatric discourse' (p. 43). A discourse has 'its own rules of appearance' (p. 120). It makes its own practical connections between, for example, legal, juridical and economic processes. The argument would suggest that it is discourses which hold together social processes. But there is one small problem with this argument: it turns everything upside down and so forgets the material basis of discourses.

The project of the *Archaeology* is, then, rather a failure. It tries to describe what Foucault calls rules inside discourse as practically unifying a whole variety of processes. This is a retreat from the earlier study of the history of madness, of the asylum and psychiatric discourse, and, even more, from the one key advance in the *Archaeology*: the entry of the argument that discourses exist materially as well as institutionally. In *The Order of Discourse* (1971, trans. 1981), where Foucault again attempted to describe discourses generally, some new directions are taken. At the same time, this work holds on to the advance made in the *Archaeology*, using it as the basis for very suggestive argument not about rules, but about the controls which act upon discourse from outside or inside it. The main proposal, which certainly bears thinking through, is that there are a number of controls which prevail upon discourse 'to gain mastery' over its 'formidable materiality' (p. 52).

Foucault's account in *The Order of Discourse* begins by sketching some of the controls which act on discourse from outside. Examples given of these are prohibitions, and the kinds of major divisions which privilege reason by condemning madness, or which set up the reign of truth by opposing it to what is false (pp. 52–4). These he calls, in a phrase which might suggest such controls act mainly to censor discourse, 'systems of exclusion' (p. 55); however, their action is not only interdictory, for they also enforce the reign of reason and of truth. Examples given of controls which work on discourse from the inside are commentary, the author and the discipline (pp. 57–9). In addition to these, his sketch outlines a third group: procedures of discursive 'subjection' or, in other words, ways to control and distribute who may speak or come within what discourse (pp. 61–4). This sketch is unlike anything in the *Archaeology*, giving a different sense of how discourses may be regulated. It posits, in effect, a series of constraints which, from inside or outside, act upon discourses and subject individuals to them.

What is interesting is the initial hypothesis that some such controls are in force mastering discourse in its 'formidable materiality' (p. 52). Although Foucault's argument here is not very specific, the most helpful way of reading *The Order of Discourse* is to understand this 'materiality' as in part composing the struggles (traversing institutions) where discourses are produced as weapons: 'as history constantly teaches us, discourse is not simply that which translates struggles or systems of domination, but is the thing for which and by which there is struggle' (pp. 52–3).

The importance of the argument, then, is to indicate two

types of processes through which discourses are constructed: discourses emerge and function as a means of struggle and, at the same time, a series of controls master and constrain discourses. Such a distinction comes close to, and adds to, that worked out so well in the ISAs essay for ideologies, between how ideologies are set up antagonistically and how prevailing practices reimpose divisions which supervene on and control their field. To bring it closer, we would have to take a more clearly materialist stand and so grasp the struggles around discourses from the ultimately antagonistic relations of class struggle, from the contradictions in which different discourses are set up. We would also have to question whether prevailing controls are all there is, prevailing in isolation. The argument may need some rethinking.

Even so, it can help alert us to the way that certain prevailing controls move to exert a mastery over the circulation even of discourses which at root are opposed to what prevails. The idealist value of the true or the figure of the author are fabricated from certain practical supports, so that authorship, for example, as a control on the circulation of discourse, is connected with bourgeois laws of property. There is a detailed study of this, in relation to films, in Edelman, *Ownership of the Image* (1973, trans. 1979). Such controls have many effects, one of which is to promote the re-entry of traditional themes into texts and discourses which have denounced them. This is argued in Foucault's essay, 'What Is an Author?' (1969, coll. 1977a, pp. 131–6). It is also, one might say, demonstrated in the self-unifying statements of his later writings, for example, in the opening of 'The Subject and Power':

> I would like to say, first of all, what has been the goal of my work during the last twenty years. It has not been to analyze the phenomena of power, nor to elaborate the foundations of such an analysis.
> My objective, instead, has been to create a history of

the different modes by which, in our culture, human beings are made subjects. (1982, p. 208)

In discourse that takes a critical stand, or goes further and takes a revolutionary stand, the effects of such controls are to be forestalled, their hold weakened as far as possible, rather than ignored.

These arguments indirectly raise the question of the 'role of the intellectual' in discursive or ideological struggles. In 'Intellectuals and Power' (1972, coll. 1977a), Foucault disposes of some obvious answers. It cannot be simply to educate: 'In the most recent upheaval' of May 1968, 'the intellectual discovered that the masses no longer need him to gain knowledge' (p. 207). Nor can it be to confer a true consciousness replacing a false consciousness: for 'consciousness as the basis of subjectivity is a prerogative of the bourgeoisie' (p. 208). Instead, Foucault suggests that the intellectual's role can be to 'sap power' in an 'activity conducted alongside those who struggle for power' (p. 208). Such a suggestion could be taken up in several ways. But its key use, I would argue, is to position: to propose that from the side of, from alongside those who struggle for power, the intellectual can engage in struggle to reveal and undermine what is most invisible and insidious in prevailing practices. From such a position, we are recalled to what is spelt out in various of Althusser's essays: that ideological and discursive struggle is not autonomous – resistance and revolutionary action at this level is work on and against what upholds existing relations of power and what keeps the working class down through subjection. This raises a further question about the part discourses have in subjecting people. I will come to that question in the next chapter.

So far, my discussion has tended to show how Foucault's archaeological writings are put together. It has used them to challenge certain idealist themes, as well as to indicate their limits as counter-discourse. Some of the points made here will be taken up rather differently in the following chapter, where the initial concern will be with questions of subjection and discourse. In relation to these questions, the studies made by Foucault in the seventies will be deployed, wherever possible, positively and directly.

6

Subjection, discourse, power

From a materialist standpoint, any explanation of discourse in terms of the speaker's personal feelings and motives will tend to mislead. Interest in subjective factors blinds us to what, in comparison, may seem a minor irrelevance: the society in which we live is one based in exploitation. Even more, such interest blinds us to the possibility of change. If, instead, the little fact of exploitation is considered first, it becomes clear that discourse is not subjective and, indeed, that individuals exist as 'subjects' because they are subjected, held to and dependent on something of an imaginary identity. Although this point was argued in chapter 2, not all the problems raised were resolved there. How are people subjected? What part do discourses have in assigning us to our places? What is this subjection? These questions can enable a fuller consideration of the ways in which discourses are constructed.

What has been argued of ideology and discourse in chapters 2 and 3 allows one to say that ideologies have a material existence, discourses are part of the ideological sphere, and ideologies are practices which subject. So that this argument may be developed, I would like, first of all, to recall what has been staked out. No ideology (no practical system of actions, meanings and beliefs) exists by itself: ideologies take shape in relation to each other. They take shape antagonistically, through the struggles which traverse various institutions, various apparatuses of the State. These struggles are connected, however indirectly, to class struggle rooted, in the last instance, in the relations of production; and it is through being pinned down, recurrently, in these struggles that discourses find their meanings.

This account lacks a theory of the part discourses have in subjection. To posit a single and general mechanism, which can be the essence of all subjection, would not help to supply this omission, for it would lead us into idealism. Instead, an advance can probably be made if we turn to historically existing modes and procedures of subjection and find out what place discourse has within them. In this respect, the analysis made by Foucault of discipline and other procedures of subjection, particularly in *Discipline and Punish* (1975, trans. 1977b), is exemplary and can be drawn upon extensively.

Subjection and the body

In the day-to-day running of institutions, discipline trains, individualizes, regiments, makes docile and obedient subjects. Whether in the school, factory or hospital, many people become caught within all the regulations, timetabling and examinations by which discipline is imposed. Foucault's analysis of discipline leaves little doubt that it is 'a subtle, calculated technology of subjection' (p. 221).

Such subjection takes in people's bodies. Foucault's studies reveal how much it is through the body that techniques of subjection find their hold; for example, discipline takes effect at 'the point where power reaches into the very grain of individuals, touches their bodies and inserts itself into their actions and attitudes, their discourses, learning processes and everyday lives' (1975a, coll. 1980a, p. 39). While subjection takes in the body, it also takes in something else.

The statement that 'ideological subjection' is 'the practical relations to body, language and thought' (Pêcheux 1983, p. 33) seems to me to offer a materialist definition and to specify what else is involved. It is somewhat cryptic. Spelt out fully, it may first of all recall that ideologies and the subjections they effect are relational: they are ultimately, but not at all exclusively, class practices. Second, it can indicate that subjection connects processes of meaning and bodies.

For a working concept of what subjection consists in and ties together, we may understand subjection as the connecting of bodies and processes of meaning, belief, etc., within the practices of class and other struggles. Forms of subjection do not all come to control; some come about as means of resistance. Foucault's researches, however, can tell us most about those which are instruments of control and means through which the power of the dominant class is developed and exercised.

Discipline is, one might say, bourgeois. Something more of its place in the social whole can be sketched out along lines familiar from the ISAs essay. It would not be wrong to consider that capitalism 'gave rise to' discipline, nor to label the techniques of disciplinary subjection as a bourgeois invention to 'assure its hegemony' (Foucault 1975, trans. 1977b, p. 221, and 1977d, coll. 1980a, p. 156). Even so, we need to notice that procedures of subjection 'do not merely constitute the "terminal" of more fundamental mechanisms' of the economy (Foucault 1982, p. 213). They have a relative autonomy and, within this, Foucault's research suggests, as does the ISAs essay, that their principal connection with the base is one of helping to secure (or, it should be added, to unsecure) its reproduction. Under capitalism, discipline is part of what makes possible, from inside and outside production (for example from both the factory and the school), the body's 'constitution as labour power' (1975, trans. 1977b, p. 26). However, where Foucault's research concentrates on labour power, the ISAs essay takes up not just additionally but in the first place the relations of production. This is a difference to which I will return.

Besides discipline, Foucault describes two other procedures

of subjection connected with sovereign power and the rule of law, both belonging to the eighteenth century. Before turning to the details of these, I should point out that his study relates each of the three procedures to a form of punishment. Like Althusser, Foucault does not see the domination of one class over another as effected merely by a coercive State apparatus (which he calls simply the State apparatus) whose police, courts, army act with a more-or-less exposed violence: 'There is a sort of schematism that needs to be avoided here – and which incidentally is not to be found in Marx – that consists of locating power in the State apparatus, making this into the major, privileged, capital and almost unique instrument of the power of one class over another' (1976, coll. 1980a, p. 72). The ISAs essay indicates the route out of such schematism. It comes to terms not only with the existence of a repressive State apparatus, but also with that of various ideological State apparatuses. But it does perhaps try to maintain too clear a distinction between violent force exerted on the body and procedures of ideological subjection, as if the latter simply hail or call into place. Pêcheux suggests that Foucault's analysis can correct this (1982, coll. 1982, p. 219), for one effect of his study of links between punishment and subjection is to tend to question, often quite disturbingly, 'the violence-ideology opposition' (Foucault 1975, trans. 1977b, p. 28). While not the same, punishment and subjection are probably not always far removed. The latter, we may say, acts by means of the body, but without the body as target.

The account of 'sovereign torture', with which *Discipline and Punish* begins, describes a practice in which an extreme of violence was combined with ideological subjection. In France, which is the focus of Foucault's study, this practice persisted well into the eighteenth century as a public spectacle of killing through which sovereign power was exercised. Torture was violent and lethal. His account suggests how it was also an ideological ritual which subjected, even as it maimed and killed, the victim, subjecting at the same time the people summoned as spectators. It did so by forcing the body of the condemned to signify.

In the ritual of torture, the body and processes of meaning were forcibly connected: 'the condemned man published his crime and the justice that had been meted out to him by bearing them physically on his body' (1975, trans. 1977b, p. 43). The violence was varied in its type, intensity and duration, according to the circumstances of the crime; it was decided by 'a legal code' and, in this way, could be adjusted to fit the crime (p. 34). So the body of the condemned was forced to signify the crime committed. At the same time, it was as a display of absolute power that the very excess of violence in the spectacle was meaningful, for torture was part of 'a policy of terror: to make everyone aware, through the body of the criminal, of the unrestrained presence of the sovereign' (p. 49). This account indicates that the spectacle of violence found its meanings both in the law and in monarchic power.

It would be idealist to suppose that, in France or other European countries, sovereign torture met its end and what is often called penal reform was born out of 'a new sensibility' (p. 82). Foucault's study locates the birth of 'penal reform' in the later eighteenth century within bourgeois class struggles against monarchic power and against popular illegalities (p. 87). While the extreme atrocities were removed, punishment became that much more generalized.

Though more restrained in its violence, punishment was to become no less conjoined with an ideological subjection. Foucault's account of penal reform concentrates on its initial proposals and projects and how these aimed at 'requalifying individuals' as 'juridical subjects' (p. 130). Penalties were calculated to reform and bring the offender back within society: for example, the vagabond who had offended by 'laziness' must be punished by being 'forced to work' (p. 106). Whereas the spectacle of torture subjected to the law as instrument of sovereign power, the projects of penal reform were aimed at subjecting to the law as both 'the contract' and 'the laws of society' (p. 89).

Even these brief sketches of the practice of torture under the feudal regime and of subsequent projects of penal reform have much to suggest. Rather than some general form of every subjection, what they suggest is the possibility of different subjections working in different ways and formed according to particular historical struggles. Moreover, they tell of the lack of a clear divide between violence and subjection, as the latter comes to connect, in no set way, bodies and ideological processes of meaning. Foucault's account covers rather more than this, and, in particular, the part of discourse, of speech and writing, in practices of subjection will be taken up in the next section. But it does little to show that others in society, besides offenders, are subjected. This is made clear, however, in the third example of punishment he describes, the penitentiary, or rather in the procedure of disciplinary subjection that combines with it. Detention in the prison quickly became, in spite of the projects of penal reform, the standard means across Europe and in America of punishing the vast majority of crimes. In the prison, the techniques of regulated and timetabled activity, silence, exercise and work were, Foucault argues, there to produce an 'obedient subject, the individual subjected to habits, rules, orders' (p. 128). These are some of the techniques of what he calls 'discipline'.

If these techniques have affected a great many people other than prisoners, that is because they have not been limited to the prison. Foucault's research patiently takes apart the disciplining which, beginning in the seventeenth and eighteenth centuries, has been introduced in the school, the hospital, the factory and the army. What I will take from his work is its broad outlines of discipline as a procedure of ideological subjection which incorporates a small, finely spread coercion.

The discipline introduced was a 'training' of the body

(p. 166). Foucault's study specifies its main principles as the control of movement and of the timing and space of activities. The body, in marching, in handling and firing a rifle, could be put through a precise sequence of movements, and 'good handwriting' made to rest upon a whole art of posture (p. 152). In discipline, there began to be procured a minute control of gesture, behaviour and activity so that the body could be conditioned to become 'more obedient as it becomes more useful' (p. 138). Besides movement, the timing and succession of activities and the space they might occupy were regulated in detail. In factories and schools, the available space was split up so that discipline could be imposed first of all when workers were allotted to different stages of the production process, or when schoolchildren were arranged in 'rows or ranks' (p. 146). Discipline puts people in 'their' places.

But the discipline introduced was more than a 'coercion of bodies' (p. 169). Disciplinary spaces from the start were not just physical. In the factory, the place to which each worker was allotted was also an operation, a job, that could characterize her or him. The ranking of pupils in school or their passage through graded tasks was joined to an assessment that could decide what abilities they might have and how good they are. Such disciplinary spaces are both real and imaginary: they bring people's bodies together with those 'characterizations, assessments, hierarchies' which decide who they are (p. 148). In this way, 'each individual has his own place, and each place its individual' (p. 143).

Indeed, what Foucault calls 'discipline' is something that at the same time '"makes" individuals' and 'normalizes' (pp. 170, 183). It has done so very much by means of surveillance and assessment. Surveillance, the supervisor's gaze, has been the coercive means with which to regulate the behaviour of workers or pupils and to judge the 'whole indefinite domain of the non-conforming' (pp. 178–9). The examination, on the other hand, is a means with which to impose a normal range

of ability, a common standard, and within this to mark
'individual differences': it is a 'pinning down of each
individual' with a mark of his or her identity (p. 192).

What Foucault's studies suggest is that discipline as a
procedure of subjection does indeed tie each individual to an
identity. Discipline probably remains one of the main
procedures in what he calls 'the government of individualization' (1982, p. 212). But we should not mistake what this
means: 'it is not that ... the individual is amputated,
repressed, altered by our social order, it is rather that the
individual is carefully fabricated in it', and not least by the
'petty, malicious minutiae of the disciplines' and the surveillance and assessment accompanying them (1975, trans. 1977b,
pp. 217, 226). His research into the disciplinary techniques,
which became prevalent in the eighteenth century and are still
much in control, can dispose of those extreme simplifications
which, mirroring each other, suppose either that individuals
are mere illusions or that they are natural beings. The
humanism which is so pleased to announce that we all share a
common nature within which we differ as individuals is a
fiction with a practical support: 'The individual is no doubt
the fictitious atom of an "ideological" representation of
society'; but the individual is also put together, 'fabricated',
by existing practices (p. 194).

If such discipline constructs individuals subjected to
bourgeois norms, it does something else besides this.
Foucault's study of prison discipline indicates that it excludes
those who cannot be brought to conform. It is a means to
divide and rule: that is, to split up those who are ruled. His
account concentrates on the prison as a site, from the end of
the eighteenth century, combining punishment with the
'disciplinary mechanisms that the new class power was
developing' in Europe and America (p. 231). Prison discipline
has never been an obvious success: those who have passed
through it have been more likely to emerge as 'delinquents',
loyal to a criminal association, than as well-disciplined

individuals (p. 266). He argues that, in this production of delinquents, the prison has paradoxically found its function: which is to exclude. The prison became a means of forming offenders into a manageable group of delinquents who might be kept under 'a constant surveillance' extending beyond the prison walls (p. 278). As such, it has been a weapon in bourgeois class struggle against the masses, a continuing means of splitting up the masses, organizing those who are not workers and opposing them to workers so that they do 'not act as a spearhead for popular resistance' (1972, coll. 1980a, p. 15).

Prison discipline, under a surveillance which ties to a criminal record and constructs the delinquent 'within a clearly demarcated, card-indexed milieu' (1975a, coll. 1980a, p. 42), excludes the non-conforming. From what has been argued here, drawing on Foucault's detailed researches, we may consider that there have been and are different forms of subjection. They may all incorporate some varying degree of coercion, acting on the body to connect it with processes of meaning. But not only do the meanings change; the methods of attaching them change as well. The techniques of discipline do not torture or brand the body to make it signify. Instead, they distribute bodies to various places and activities. They prescribe the body's movements, impose norms on its activity, watch out for any deviation, and exclude the non-conforming. In these ways, the body is connected with processes of meaning: it is tied to an identity, a level of ability, the specifications of a job, a criminal record.

The ISAs essay broke new ground in understanding the ideological practices of subjection which exist antagonistically and take shape in struggle. Foucault's study makes an important advance in detailing certain practices of subjection. Even so, it has some gaps and I will return to these in a later section. In particular, its way of focusing on what prevails and comes to control those who are ruled might seem in parts rather blind to the bases of revolt and resistances – although he does mention that the people sometimes tried to resist the spectacle of sovereign torture, while his account of penal reform tends to suggest this emerged in struggle from a position opposing monarchic power, one disidentifying with it. But his study can also add much to our understanding of specifically verbal discourse, speech and writing. By taking further those instances of ideological subjection which have been described, we may be able to see ways in which such practices place and limit discourses – and, conversely, ways in which discourses contribute not only to these subjections but also to their resistance. Again, there will be some gaps.

Discourse and subjection

Working from the ISAs essay and using materialist propositions, Pêcheux has argued that discourses, which have a basis in language, are none the less part of the ideological sphere and are set up in relation to each other, antagonistically. A discourse finds its meanings by reference to an ideological position: it is pinned down where it serves as a weapon in struggle. These arguments were put forward in chapter 3. Many issues concerning the material existence of discourse were considered there; but some of these, notably the practical effects of discourse as a direct or indirect instrument of subjection, were touched upon only briefly.

Discourse can be a direct instrument of ideological subjection. For example, schoolchildren write in examinations the words they have learned; these are used to mark them. Their words subject them according to how much their answers conform to or stray from the questions. Foucault's studies can help to substantiate and develop earlier arguments, for they make visible some effects of discourse within practices of subjection. While having less to say about discourse that is fully antagonistic to what prevails, they tell us much about effects of prevailing discourse and discourse countering it on the same terrain.

First, prevailing discourse. In the ritual of sovereign torture, the body, branded with violence, was forced to signify the justice of the punishment. In addition, the speech of the condemned or the writing attached to him also announced the truth of such justice and subjected him to it. A discourse was assigned to him, and its words were meaningful in relation to the law and sovereign power condemning him in the ritual. Foucault's account describes how it was that the 'guilty man' became 'the herald of his own condemnation' – through 'the placard attached to his back, chest or head as a reminder of the sentence', through 'the *amende honorable*' he was required to make, through the words he was called upon to speak, the condemned confessed his crime and guilt and the justice of his punishment (1975, trans. 1977b, p. 43). There was much to encourage confession, not least the chance of a last-minute pardon, for even at the foot of the scaffold those condemned could gain a respite if they had 'further revelations to make' (p. 53).

Using Pêcheux's concepts, we can see in the confession, placard, and *amende honorable* 'freely consented to' by the guilty man, an 'identification' with his condemnation by the law and the sovereign (1975, trans. 1982, pp. 156–7). Foucault cites as an example of 'the good condemned man' François Billiard who murdered his wife in 1772. 'The executioner wanted to hide his face to spare him the insults of the crowd: "This punishment, which I have merited, has not been inflicted upon me," he said, "so that I should not be seen by the public ..."' (1975, trans. 1977b, p. 44). Such identification, a little ambiguous no doubt but utterly complicit, was what discourse could effect in the public spectacle of execution.

To go further, we may well need to consider that the spectacle of torture and execution took shape as a weapon against the practices of popular resistance: it was a public spectacle (behind locked doors it would have been different) and one in which the prevailing discourse was there to silence and rule out the discourse and practice of popular resistance. From this standpoint, we can begin to grasp that the prevailing discourse could be countered, but not overthrown, by anything keeping to its terms and its terrain. What could speak beside it, on its terrain, was a counter-discourse which, Foucault's description suggests, took the monarchic order of condemnation and reversed it. Often, instead of insults, the people would give 'shouts of encouragement' to the one haled to execution who, instead of condemning himself, would 'curse the judges, the laws, the government and religion', and sometimes the spectacle, so turned about, could end in riot (p. 60). Again using Pêcheux's concepts, we can see, in this reversal and counter-discourse, the opening up of a 'counter-identification' with the exercise of power in the spectacle (1975, trans. 1982, pp. 157–8).

Still tending to focus on what prevailed, Foucault's study indicates that words used after the event could also be part of the practice of subjection. For example, around the spectacle of the execution, even street literature such as broadsheets, which recounted 'the "last words of a condemned man"', could find their meanings in the exercise of power: they furnished the required confessions and 'proofs' of justice (1975, trans. 1977b, p. 66). But in the broadsheets, prevailing discourse could again and to a further degree be reversed; and, even while their circulation was encouraged as an 'ideological control', the avid reading of such fictional confessions of crimes could be practised in search of 'precedents' (p. 68). From his brief sketch, it would seem that the equivocal use in the broadsheets of words such as 'misfortune' and 'abomination' and 'famous' and 'lamentable' (the latter for the death) brought these texts near to being a battleground between opposing discourses (p. 68). However, his account describes no more than this: it gives us no instance of a popular discourse which, taking shape both against and from beyond the terrain of what prevailed, could effect what Pêcheux calls 'disidentification' (1975, trans. 1982, pp. 158–9).

Instead, it indicates the emergence of some thoroughly bourgeois literature which came to undercut, not the confession but the popular heroism of crime. From the end of the eighteenth century there began to develop a literature of crime in which the criminal, rather than appearing as a woman or man of and for the people, became someone of bourgeois origins and 'an enemy of the poor' (Foucault 1975a, coll. 1980a, p. 46). One could say that such literature brought about disidentification with the populist appeal of the broadsheets. None the less, the revaluation it gave to crime – as the 'exclusive privilege of those who are really great' (1975, trans. 1977b, pp. 68–9) – was an element in a new prevailing discourse which, as a weapon in bourgeois class struggle against the masses, related to the splitting up of workers and criminals brought about by prison discipline. That various elements in this discourse were reversed by a counter-discourse is again marked out in Foucault's study. On the one hand, the split between criminals and workers was identified with and accepted in workers' newspapers, for example, in their campaigns against the 'comfort of the prisons' (pp. 286–7). On the other hand, the workers' newspapers would often reverse, term by term, the prevailing discourse; Foucault cites *L'Humanitaire*, August 1841: 'The man who kills you is not free not to kill you. It is society or, to be more precise, bad social organization that is responsible' (p. 287).

On discourse and subjection, Foucault's studies have most to say about the effects of discourse in forms of subjection which prevail and come to control, and they tell us little about discourse which, rather than merely countering, is able to bring about disidentification and a change of terrain. So they leave out much of that antagonistic setting up of discourses which Pêcheux's more materialist theory is orientated towards, and only just begin to notice that words can change their meanings with the positions from which they are used. What these studies do make visible, and can indeed help us to dismantle, is the acceptance and reversal of prevailing discourse. In displaying ways in which discourse, as an instrument in prevailing forms of subjection, has been repeated or reversed, they can give substance to arguments about the 'symmetry' of identification and counter-identification (see Pêcheux 1975, trans. 1982, p. 157). To change what prevailed, they seem to suggest, more was and is needed: discourse and action (at one time bourgeois, but now no longer) that is revolutionary.

So far, some notice has been taken of direct effects of discourses in practices of subjection, but not of their less direct effects. These may be quite important: in particular, discourses may often provide such practices with a kind of backing. For example, the so-called 'sciences of man', which are, as knowledges, at once discursive and technical, have backed the effect of discipline in normalizing individuals. So, since the nineteenth century, 'the supervision of normality' has been 'firmly encased in a medicine or a psychiatry that provided it with a sort of "scientificity"' (Foucault 1975, trans. 1977b, p. 296). Criminology, psychology and other 'biographical' knowledges which delight our humanity have also, one might say, found their place here.

These 'human sciences' (together with other knowledges and 'serious' discourses) exist among what may be called the theoretical ideologies. Keeping to a materialist route, we may approach them cautiously and from a stage beforehand by using Lecourt's very neat formulation: 'practical ideologies assign theoretical ideologies their forms and their limits' (1972, trans. 1975, p. 211). Its shorthand can recall much that has already been argued, not least in chapter 3. Practical ideologies (as procedures which subject) are rooted and take shape in class and other struggles, and it is through the practical ideologies that these struggles come to define the domains of knowledge, serious discourse, etc. As part of this process, knowledges find much of their meanings and effects by reference to the practical ideologies.

This is perhaps oversimplified in Foucault's suggestion that knowledge is determined in its forms and domains by the 'struggles that traverse it' (1975, trans. 1977b, p. 28). None the less, much of this is given substance by his studies. He takes criminology as an example, an extreme one, of a discourse formed to justify disciplinary subjection, or, rather, less that whole group of ideological devices which he calls discipline, than the specific discipline of the prison. Criminology was, he points out, urgently required by the excuse given for prison discipline, by the 'alibi, employed since the eighteenth century, that if one imposes a penalty on somebody this is not in order to punish what he has done, but to transform what he is' (1975a, coll. 1980a, p. 47). Indeed, so urgently was it required that its knowledge was formed with no coherent framework and none has been acquired since. What criminology supports is at once the promise and the failure of prison discipline, for judges can tell 'perfectly well that the instruments available to them', detention and the prison, 'don't transform anyone'. Its discourse has been called forth to 'justify the measures in question' (p. 48). By continual failure, prison discipline gives the bourgeoisie a means of subjecting and dividing the masses. And criminology, his account suggests, has arisen to supply this discipline with a pretext, in order to forget the failure in a knowledge which can have the effect of controlling criticism of the prison. As Foucault says, the bourgeoisie is 'intelligent and cynical' (p. 47).

Not only criminology, but also psychiatry, psychology and the 'human sciences', back the workings of discipline. They have effects as well in other spheres of social practice. But this little sketch of criminology can nicely suggest that the way to approach them (in order to recognize how they obstruct radical criticism) is through their relation to practical ideology. To use Althusser's formulation, these knowledges, these theoretical ideologies are 'in the last instance "detachments" of the practical ideologies in the theoretical field' (1973, coll. 1976b, p. 37).

Besides alerting us to the effects of these knowledges, Foucault's study has something to say about the techniques they use. In the process of backing discipline, these knowledges acquire many of their techniques from its workings. In particular, his account suggests how important examination and surveillance have been to the constitution of the human sciences. The techniques of examination, whether in defining individual aptitudes or in dealing with patients, along with the records, files and registrations which a continuous surveillance deploys, have proved indispensable here: such techniques have made it possible to form 'the individual as a describable, analysable object' (1975, trans. 1977b, p. 190). In fact, in *Discipline and Punish*, his account builds rather much on that 'technical matrix' of these knowledges (p. 226) and too little on the effects (so sharply sketched for criminology in 'Prison Talk') through which they are ultimately caught up in struggles.

Foucault's subsequent studies again describe some reverse discourse. The discourse of the human sciences has not stood by itself, unquestioned. On a major scale, it has been radically opposed through working-class struggle and through Marxist science and philosophy. But there have also been localized challenges, and one of these, dating from the end of the nineteenth century, is picked up in Foucault's studies of sexuality. (Those studies are in many ways differently based, increasingly so; but the instance of a nineteenth-century reversal does tie in with the earlier examples.)

His account considers first the human sciences. In making individuals, examination and surveillance have been used to fit people out with a sexual identity. These identities have been set up along a division between the normal and the perverse. The human sciences, especially psychology and psychiatry, have had an active part in what Foucault calls a 'perverse implantation': making perversion become inner nature 'everywhere present' in an individual (1976, trans. 1979, pp. 43–4). He takes the example of homosexuality. In the ways in which this category was put together (as a 'psychological, psychiatric, medical category') around the 1870s, the homosexual 'became a personage, a past, a case history, and a childhood, in addition to being a type of life, a life form' (p. 43).

What he suggests is that the discursive categorizing of homosexuality in part 'made possible the formation of a "reverse" discourse' (p. 101). This turned the same words and often the same arguments into a challenge. Its effect was that 'homosexuality began to speak in its own behalf, to demand that its legitimacy or "naturality" be acknowledged' (p. 101). Foucault's rather imprecise description would seem to indicate that this reverse discourse was made up of a mixture both of something more and of something less than a simple negation. On the one hand, a repetition amounting to acceptance of homosexuality as a personal identity; and, on the other hand, an appropriation consisting in turning to advantage this imposed identity. It was a reversal saying in effect, 'all right, we are what you say we are, by nature, illness or perversion, as you wish. Well, if we are what you say, let's be it, and if you want to know what we are we'll tell you ourselves better than you can' (1977, trans. 1980b, p. 7).

This short example can help us to recognize the main features of reverse discourses: they are held in a kind of symmetry, which consists in resisting only within, and on the terrain of, the prevailing ideologies they would challenge. But where a divide is all set up and imposed at the ideological level, through what prevails, this may be the only form of contestation within it. For homosexual discourse and homosexual identity, as effects of an imposed divide splitting the normal from the abnormal, there may be no other resistance. To go any further would be to start on the task of dismantling that identity – which is what Foucault's study does.

But in *The History of Sexuality*, volume 1, the same example is also used as part of a project to question whether reversal may be the mechanism of all resistances. That project leads away from any materialist arguments; it is a retreat. Since it informs much of the text, and the bases of his writing are shifted, radical opposition to the human sciences is by and large discounted. There is no sense of the antagonistic setting up of discourses. For example, the radical opposition between the discourses of the human sciences and of Marxism, and the disidentification which the latter brings about, is not taken up. Some analogous gaps in Foucault's preceding researches have already been mentioned. These gaps are not failures of empirical study; they are the blind points of his writing, of the tendency in it towards pragmatism.

Of power and resistance, or, What's wrong with pragmatism

In brief, one could say pragmatism is whatever proposes simply that practice has primacy over theory. Materialism proposes this as well, and yet there is a conflict between them. Whereas pragmatism starts out from this proposition, materialism places before it material contradictions, real relations, such as the basic economic relations between capitalists and wage-earners. They tend to get lost in pragmatism.

Many of Foucault's writings from 1971 to 1975 have links with the work of the Groupe d'Information sur les Prisons (see chapter 1). There is much in these texts tending towards materialism, and, wherever possible, they have been considered from this standpoint in my arguments. But there is also much that pulls towards a kind of pragmatism; and this comes increasingly to dominate Foucault's writings of the later seventies. It is worth noting immediately that even in their pragmatism these writings do not rule out struggle; they make it secondary and consider it in the form of a contest or competition. Sometimes from this standpoint, we are given a quite subjective view of a kind of drama acted out by individuals or groups. In *I, Pierre Rivière* (1973, trans. 1978), the documents of the Rivière trial are looked at as a 'contest' or, rather, 'several separate combats' among Rivière himself, the judges and prosecution, and the psychiatrists (p. x). Moreover, sometimes what is displayed to us as struggles are rituals within a practice: *Discipline and Punish* includes some description of the practice of public execution as a ritualized contest at the heart of which was a 'struggle' between 'the criminal and the sovereign' (1975, trans. 1977b, p. 50). What this perspective cannot grasp are the antagonistic relations in which practices take shape as weapons of struggle.

Many noticeable inconsistencies in Foucault's writings are effects, in part, of the combined pull of materialism and pragmatism upon them. For example, in 'Prison Talk' Foucault suggests that his studies are situated 'within a horizon of thought which has been defined and described by Marx' (1975a, coll. 1980a, p. 53). But in 'Body/Power', he says, 'I think I would distinguish myself from both the Marxist and the para-Marxist perspectives' (1975b, coll. 1980a, p. 58). Since these writings are bound together in books circulating under Foucault's name, we cannot come upon their tendency towards materialism without encountering also the pragmatism that increasingly departs from this. I want to turn now to some effects of that departure, and then to his theory of power and resistance on which, most of all, it leaves its mark.

Some gaps in Foucault's study of discipline have been mentioned already. His account focuses on the training of the body. It tells us much about the means of impressing a variety of skills and aptitudes, which can make anybody into an individual worker fitted for capitalist production. It tells us also how prison discipline is used to exclude some among the masses who cannot be brought to conform. But it tells us nothing about the subjection of the bourgeoisie or about working-class struggle. The tendency towards pragmatism in his account brings it to a halt before these.

Anybody can be disciplined; but not everybody ends up simply as a worker or, in the eyes of the law, a criminal. Foucault's study is inclined to overlook this and give the misleading idea that the bourgeoisie is somehow outside discipline and unsubjected. Yet in education, for example, discipline is not confined to just one sector: to take the British case, it is as prevalent in public-independent schools as in comprehensives. Although it is a bourgeois weapon, it is not only impressed on the masses. In detailing the techniques of discipline in and by themselves, Foucault's study creates a problem here and makes discipline seem altogether one-sided: the 'subordination of one group of people by another' (1975, trans. 1977b, p. 223). To correct this, one would probably need to consider how discipline, where it acts on everyone (for example, in schools), is bound up with prevailing practices which do impose divisions along class lines.

The omission of workers' or popular struggle is a more serious problem. Discipline is, as he indicates, a means through which the power of the dominant class is exercised. None the less, his account tends to suggest this power exists by itself and on its own terms. Indeed, his description runs the risk of marking out the 'ideal' of discipline, in which the schoolchild, soldier, worker become fully trained, blindly obedient bodies, like domesticated animals or, rather, like robots. In this bad dream, what prevails is all there is. Again, this problem is the result of the pragmatist tendency to suppose that a practice can emerge outside of contradiction and struggle. Fortunately, discipline is not so simple for the bourgeoisie: the work-force, for a start, is not so blindly obedient.

Thus there are problems. Even so, Foucault's studies in the early seventies are far from immaterial in what they indicate about discourses and practices of subjection; and the extent to which they can give substance to materialist arguments has been outlined in the preceding sections. But the problems, instead of being resolved, are intensified in his later writings, as these lay down increasingly pragmatic guidelines for studying power and resistance in what might be called the ideological sphere. The results of this are that his later writings come to have the damaging political effect of making revolt altogether unthinkable and they turn their back on advances in the study of discourse.

Foucault's comments on power are a mixture of definitions and directions. From the start, their mistake is to suppose that all choices are simple: if one argument is wrong, another must be right. A standard argument is that power is mainly repressive. Foucault replaces this with the suggestion that power is mainly 'productive' (1977b, coll. 1980a, p. 119), and is exercised much more in forms of 'control' than in forms of 'prohibition' (1976, trans. 1979, p. 41). If we consider how power is exercised through ideological means, such as discipline, this statement makes some sense: discipline, as his studies show, is an insidious means of producing and controlling individuals. But this suggestion does little to help us consider how power is at work in the deadly forces of physical repression, especially the army and the police. Perhaps power is *both* repressive *and* productive.

Likewise, it is standard to argue that power is an actual thing, a distinct entity, and instead Foucault states that 'power means relations' (1977e, coll. 1980a, p. 198). However, there can be more than one kind of relation. His explanation of what is involved attends only to the relation inside power (how power dominates by subordinating), which he calls the 'relationship' with 'the one over whom power is exercised' (1982, p. 220). It misses any relation between power and resistance. Specifically, it misses any antagonistic relation in which the means of power take shape against resistance, as they do if both are rooted, in the last instance, in class struggle set up through the economy.

His explanation, looking only at the 'inside' of power, is linked to his major and most damaging guideline. This asks us to suppose that, 'power *is* "always already there"' on its own terms (1977c, coll. 1980a, p. 141). In other words, what prevails is all there is: power is made up only of an 'inside'. For actual studies, this line requires 'a non-economic analysis of power' (1977a, coll. 1980a, p. 89). Now, the crucial difficulty with these arguments is that they leave resistance in a blind alley.

The problem is perhaps overstated by Poulantzas: 'if power is always already there, if every power situation is immanent in itself, *why should there ever be resistance? From where* would resistance come, and *how would it be even possible?*' (1978, trans. 1978, p. 149). For Foucault's argument does not disallow all resistances. It still allows the reversals, reverse discourses and counter-identifications, whose limits have been indicated by his preceding studies. These may be able to form as secondary effects of the power situation itself: he suggests they can come about in the 'strategic field' of power (1976, trans. 1979, p. 96). None the less, while it may be possible to make do with this argument when studying the reversals which have a symmetry with power and which buy small gains through being (in his terms) 'the compatriot of power' (1977c, coll. 1980a, p. 142), it is impossible to go further: the argument will not let us study revolutions and radical changes. Foucault's history of sexuality does little to document any forms of resistance, and, if it accepts that there have been radical upheavals, cannot analyse these. From the point of view which sees all resistance simply as an effect of power, those revolutionary class struggles in which existing relations of power have been overthrown appear and disappear like magic.

In what might look like a move to sort out these problems, Foucault suggests another guideline: start from the local lines of force operating in any area. His move supposes we live in a pluralistic society of war: 'Who fights against whom? We all fight each other' (1977e, coll. 1980a, p. 208). What he proposes is that any study should make an 'ascending' analysis, should examine first 'the most immediate, the most local power relations at work' in a given area, and should ascend from these to what he calls 'grand strategies' of class struggle (1976, trans. 1979, p. 97; and 1977a, 1977e, coll. 1980a, pp. 99, 203). But, again, his argument presumes all choices are simple: make an 'ascending' rather than a 'descending' analysis: start from the 'local' rather than from the 'global'. No doubt the kind of analysis which he takes to be descending and global would consider the bourgeoisie as a subject whose collective consciousness and essential interests are expressed in the means of control. In other words, such an analysis, in idealist fashion, would try to figure out what can be 'deduced from the general phenomenon of the domination of the bourgeois class' (1977a, coll. 1980a, p. 100). However, his emphasis on this choice between the 'local' and the 'global' is unhelpful, for the choice is ultimately a false one in that both the methods he mentions can give precedence to power. If the analysis supposes power is always already there, no amount of attention to local tactics will indicate the basis of those revolutionary class struggles which bring about radical changes. Making the study local can only defer this impasse.

In the introductory volume of Foucault's *History of Sexuality*, some use of a local point of view does indeed defer the need to confront historical change and class struggle. But the eventual announcement that 'sexuality is originally, historically bourgeois' (1976, trans. 1979, p. 127) still enters with the force of a contradiction undercutting his proposed guidelines. In his usage here, 'sexuality' covers a complex of practical and discursive concerns with bodily vitality and health, secret desires that are the 'truth' of the self, eugenics and race. According to the little sketch he gives, these concerns first came about as a means of bourgeois class struggle, when, 'at the end of the eighteenth century, the bourgeoisie set its own body and its precious sexuality against the valorous blood of the nobles' (pp. 127–8). And later, as the arena of struggle shifted, these concerns changed: the bourgeoisie 'sought to redefine the specific character of its sexuality' against the working class (p. 128).

This argument, slightly shaky though it is, will do as an example. Because, even to notice the possibility of historical change, it has to make use of two decisive points which show the limits of his pragmatic guidelines. First, revolutionary struggle consists in more than turning round existing practices and discourses. Second, practices and discourses, whether as means of revolutionary struggle or as means of exercising power, are shaped by what they are required to work on and against. On these two points, I would argue, a stand is to be taken: a materialist stand, in which to begin to grasp how antagonistic relations of class struggle are (on any level) the motor of history.

Foucault should have changed terrain. The pragmatic standpoint, which places practice first and makes struggle secondary, cannot avoid giving precedence to power and locating resistance merely as a counter-effect in the networks of power. It thereby makes the historical existence of radical changes unthinkable. Within this position, the choice of 'local' or 'global' situations as a starting-point misses the antagonisms of class struggle, until these have to be imported, in the end, from another terrain. The work done by Althusser and Pêcheux on ideology and discourse shows how, by starting from class struggle, radical action and change can be grasped even in the ideological sphere. Starting there, their work can demonstrate that no practice or discourse exists in itself: on whatever side, it is ultimately shaped and 'preceded' by what it is opposing, and so can never simply dictate its own terms. And neither is it simply tied to terms laid down before it.

Conclusion

Detailed discussion of *The History of Sexuality* would be out of place here. But, in the eight years separating the short introductory volume from the publication, in 1984, of two further volumes, representing a meticulous study – *L'usage des plaisirs* and *Le souci de soi* – Foucault's project has undergone a dramatic revision. It becomes 'recentred . . . on the genealogy of the man of desire' (1984a, p. 18). That change prompts some notice.

Foucault's genealogy traces through texts of antiquity the evolving forms in which individuals were called 'to recognize themselves as subjects' both of sexuality and of a moral conduct (p. 10). Perhaps most instantly surprising is this change of period: his return from current concerns, across Christianity, to Greek and Roman antiquity. By this means, Foucault suggests, he has been able to ask a very simple and general question: why have sexual behaviour, activity and pleasure, been made objects of a moral preoccupation?

To examine the ancient texts of philosophy, medicine, and dream-divination, he takes up again the notion of 'discursive practices' first proposed in *The Archaeology of Knowledge*. That notion, from the start all too abstract, is now used in ways unenvisaged in the *Archaeology* to map the forming of self-consciousness, subjectivity and experience. The two-volume study is very much an attempt to monitor the internal structure of a discourse, the sexual morality of antiquity, in its problematization of certain areas – notably, the conjugal relation between husband and wife, and love for boys – and in its forming of a subject, the man of desire, and of an object, the experience of sexuality. Perhaps what makes for the disturbing blandness of Foucault's study is precisely this attempt to deal with the structure of a discourse in itself and in its forming of a single point of view. Moral cultivation or oneself, it appears, pertained only to some (Foucault does not specify precisely whom) among those who were free-born and not slaves, and among men and not women. It was an 'elaboration of masculine conduct from the point of view of men and to give form to their conduct' (p. 29), and it 'concerned only the social groups, very limited in number, who were the bearers of culture' (1984b, p. 59). It is to this discourse and point of view that Foucault confines his attention.

His arguments, curiously, present no challenge. Without insisting on a steady continuity in sexual morality from antiquity to Christianity, he suggests a gradual evolution. Noticing first that, whereas Christianity limited legitimate sexual activity to marriage and disqualified homosexual relations, antiquity recognized no such strict limits and indeed in some ways exalted same-sex relations, he none the less easily disposes of any illusion of unrestrained sexuality in ancient times. Themes of moderation and an increasing austerity, it would seem, belonged to antiquity no less than to Christianity. However, these themes did not always have the same place and value: in antiquity, austerity and moderation were not organized into a total morality to be followed by all – instead, they provided an added and superior ethos.

It appears that between classical Greek culture down to the fourth century BC and the Greek or Latin texts of the first two centuries AD, there was also a difference in emphasis which subtly altered the form of the subject of desire. Foucault isolates this evolution in the prevailing thought. At first, in earlier antiquity, the Greeks recommended certain kinds of moderation as the best and most accomplished form of conduct. Restraint in the use of pleasures seems to have been understood as a mark of a man's mastery over himself, a mastery in keeping with and appropriate to the authority which he exercised over others in the household and in the city. In the morality of later antiquity, through four themes – 'mistrust of pleasures, insistence on the effects of their abuse for the body and the soul, valorization of marriage and of conjugal obligations, disaffection with regard to the spiritual significations attributed to the love for boys' (p. 53) – he traces an increase in austerity and a development of its value. Austerity, while still linked to the self, was increasingly connected, it appears, to a whole art of living centred on concern and care for the self: 'This art of one-self is not now so insistent on the excesses one can indulge in and that one ought to master so as to exercise one's domination over others; it increasingly emphasizes the vulnerability of the individual to the various ills which can result from sexual activities' (p. 272). There is a modification, then, in representations: the morality surrounding the subject of desire bears more and more in later antiquity on the conduct appropriate to an art of living, to health and to self-respect.

Clearly, there is a departure here from Foucault's previous studies which, however ambiguous their stand, challenged prevailing views. These volumes, in comparison are regressive and flat. It seems to me that Foucault finds what it appears he wants to find: a way to analyse subjectivity, or self-consciousness, as this has been formed by discourse. But his method disengages discourse from history, and idealizes both discourse and its effects, so that he detaches both not only from the class struggle in antiquity, but also from gender and other differences worked out through ideological practices. In the event, by looking only at the free-born and ruling point of view of male dominance in antiquity, Foucault provides an analysis which takes the standard notion of the 'subject' at face value. Through his genealogy, the 'subject' appears too simply as an individual who is active in a relation to others who are the passive, subordinated objects of his desire.

Even if our distance, and the comparatively small number of remaining texts, present difficulties, there is the political issue. In his detachment of a discourse, Foucault can faithfully look, within thought, to consciousness of self and to subjectivity. He can do no more. He has left no basis from which to turn a critical gaze upon the thought he examines – or upon recent discourses which, as part of ruling class ideology, now privilege individuality and self-regard.

What gets lost here, along with the real process of history, are the effects of that process in the forming of consciousness. The consciousness of slaves, of women and men, caught up in forms of thought not simply those of male dominance, divided between identifications and disidentifications, is all set aside for the sake of this view of male subjectivity. Not everything can be put to new use. The notion of subjectivity may be unavoidably idealist.

In conclusion, I wish to take up again what seems a key term, 'disidentification', for which Foucault's studies can find no place, and from it indicate some issues for further inquiry. I have used this term to describe something which makes the forming of consciousness neither stagnant nor readily unified. What is involved appears as the effect in consciousness of the contradictions which traverse the sphere of ideology and discourse, such that, for the masses now subjected by capitalist regimes, disidentification is brought about through working on and against the dominant forms of ideological subjection. This is a question, at the level of thought, of the transformation and not the repetition of the meanings and identities dominantly imposed. What is at stake seems to be neither some 'external' triumph of an independent thought, nor some 'internal' reversal: rather, it is the taking up of antagonistic positions which have the force of a contradiction to what prevails. I have suggested that Marxist theory holds out for us precisely such a revolutionary theory and practice of disidentification. But this is not to say, of course, that this theory exists as a 'disidentification-kit' which provides an escape, just like that. Hopes of a kit are a little illusory. Rather, it would seem that in our times disidentification is possible as the continuing uncompleted outcome, in the forming of consciousness, of a dual process: Marxist theory as revolutionary theory; resistance and revolutionary class struggle in the sphere of ideology and politics. This raises several issues.

First, if this theory, in its scientific, political and ideological forms, does not have the status of some independent and ideal truth, is this to say that it cannot be developed outside of some contradiction, with consequent risks? Is disidentification, then, to be conceived as the effect of a process in which existing revolutionary theory is always put at some risk in the act of working towards the transformation of the society in which we live? One further question: is disidentification altogether an effect – or is it thereby also a force that, as it were, de-States the masses, contributing thus, in its own way, towards the seizure of power necessary to any transformation of society?

While raising these issues, I recognize the danger of reformism, which cannot be underestimated. When the ideological struggle of the ruling class is pursued within organizations and programmes of the labour movement, that is reformism. To use Althusser's phrase, it is what 'serves the political interests of the bourgeoisie, even inside the labour movement' (1973, coll. 1976b, p. 64).

'Spontaneous' resistances, forms of counter-identification, and reverse discourses, caught between complicity and challenge, would seem to be just as ambiguous as any kind of reformism. But reformism in discourse and counter-discourse are not the same: and it is a matter of some urgency to clarify, through concrete analyses, their political distinction.

In this connection, further study of reformism in discourse

is needed, again providing concrete analyses and here the lines
indicated by Pêcheux's work are probably important. It is
significant, in addition to what was discussed in chapter 3,
that the results of the experiment at the CNRS go beyond its
initial hypotheses. Pêcheux's account makes clear how the
experiment, by splitting the text of the Mansholt report,
displayed the contradictions in the text between discourse of
the Right and that of the Left, and so demonstrated
something of the ambiguity of reformist programmes. But the
results showed something more than this, as he emphasizes:
that, in the ambiguities of the text, the discourse of the Right
dominates and partly silences that of the Left around certain
crucial issues, most notably the question of State power, so
that the Left discourse, in calling for radical economic
changes, fails to specify 'the political agents necessary to
effect the proposed transformations'. In this, the Mansholt
report induces a double illusion: that such changes could be
carried out either by a bourgeois government or without
touching the question of State power. Such entry of discourse
of the Right into that of the Left 'to limit it, to distort its form
and content' is, he accordingly suggests, 'the most character-
istic sign of reformism in political and ideological struggle'
(1978, p. 260).

Notes

Introduction

1 See Davies 1978, coll. 1981, Doyle 1982 and Eagleton 1983 and 1984.

1   The end of the 1960s

1 For discussions of the events of May see Harvey 1978, Johnson 1972, Seale and McConville 1968 and Singer 1970.

2   From ideology to discourse: the Althusserian stand

1 This approach can be found even in some passages of the Marxist classics. None the less, as Macherey indicates in 'Problems of Reflection', it is affiliated to traditional philosophy and is not materialist (1977, p. 46).

2 For a detailed consideration of the 1944 Education Act, see *Unpopular Education* (Centre for Contemporary Cultural Studies 1981, pp. 57−64).

3 For example, Paul Hirst reads the essay in such a way as to assume that the ISAs *must* function on behalf of capital, making change inconceivable. His reading involves several related errors: ignoring the antagonistic existence of ideologies, he supposes ideology-in-general is realized in the ISAs that thus automatically reproduce capitalist relations (1976b, coll. 1979, pp. 42−6). Were this so, ideological struggle would be impossible. However, Althusser's argument does refute such pessimism explicitly: 'the ISAs are not the realization of ideology *in general*, nor even the conflict-free realization of the ideology of the ruling class' (1970, coll. 1971, p. 172).

4 In this, his philosophy connects with psychoanalysis and linguistics which have made some moves this century to undercut what humanism

has everyone know. An account of the connections is provided in Belsey (1980, pp. 56–67).

5 Hirst (1976b, coll. 1979, pp. 57–68) and Adlam et al. (1977, pp. 5–56) make such attempts to displace Althusser's philosophy towards a theory of subjectivity. Even Pêcheux (1975, trans. 1982) includes some rethinking, careful though it is, along these lines.

6 Summaries and examples, treated critically in part, may be found in Easthope (1983, pp. 122–9) and Belsey (1980, pp. 67–102).

3 Meaningful antagonisms: Pêcheux on discourse

1 Having separated 'language' from 'thought', Pêcheux undertakes to specify some general mechanisms for discursive thought, which he calls 'preconstruction' and the 'sustaining process'. He posits these together as the equivalent for discourse of the mechanism of ideological interpellation. The first would supply the obviousness of meanings in a world of things, and the second would constitute the subject in relation to meaning (1975, trans. 1982, pp. 115–21). But this project lapses again into what might be, if unkindly, called a science of the non-existent and so is unhelpful in a way that Pêcheux's arguments for a politics of meaning are not. It needs rethinking.

2 I have used the following edition: Burke (1793).

4 Discourse and the critique of epistemology

1 Here, and throughout, 'Hindess and Hirst' refers to writings published under either or both of these names, or both with Cutler and Hussain.

2 Easthope implies that Hindess and Hirst make these relativist and humanist assumptions (1983, p. 130). In fact, they largely avoid them.

3 Skillen finds a similar problem (1978, p. 4). It is worth adding that, although Hindess and Hirst state that objects 'must be referred to solely in and through the forms of discourse, theoretical, political, etc., in which they are specified', they do grant that 'another, critical or complementary, discourse' can refer to these objects (1977a, p. 19). However, this qualification is unexplained and is inconsistent with their other arguments.

5 Foucault's archaeologies of knowledge

1 *Madness and Civilization* is a translation of the abridged French edition (Paris: Plon, 1961). The full text was also published by Plon, under the title *Folie et déraison, Histoire de la folie à l'âge classique* (1961).

2 Important work in this field is being developed by Dominique Lecourt (see Bibliography).

Bibliography

This is not an exhaustive bibliography. Rather, it is a reference-list for the writings I have quoted and discussed, followed by brief notes on additional items. The references give, after the main title of any collection, details of the specific essays, interviews, etc. which are taken up in my discussion. Where an item has been subsequently translated into English, or published in an edited volume, dates of first publication are given in square brackets. These dates appear first in references in the text. I have asterisked those titles which a reader wishing to familiarize her/himself with the issues and theories of discourse introduced here might most usefully consult. Presence or absence of an asterisk does not imply approval or disapproval of a particular item. In the brief notes on additional pieces, I have concentrated on work available in English.

References

Adlam, Diana and Henriques, Julian and Rose, Nikolas and Salfield, Angie and Venn, Couze and Walkerdine, Valerie (1977) 'Psychology, ideology and the human subject'. *Ideology and Consciousness*, 1, 5–56.

*Althusser, Louis (1971) *Lenin and Philosophy and Other Essays*, trans. Ben Brewster. London: New Left Books. Contains:
[1968a] 'Philosophy as a Revolutionary Weapon'.
[1968b] 'Lenin and Philosophy'.
[1970] 'Ideology and Ideological State Apparatuses (Notes towards an Investigation)'.

Althusser, Louis (1976a) *Positions (1964–1975)*. Paris: Éditions Sociales. Contains:
[1971] 'Marxisme et lutte de classe'.
*Althusser, Louis (1976b) *Essays in Self-Criticism*, trans. Grahame Lock. London: New Left Books. Contains:
[1973] 'Reply to John Lewis'.
[1974] 'Elements of Self-Criticism'.
[1975] 'Is it Simple to be a Marxist in Philosophy?'
*Althusser, Louis (1978) 'What Must Change in the Party' [1978], trans. Patrick Camiller. *New Left Review*, 109, 19–45.
Althusser, Louis and Balibar, Étienne (1970) *Reading Capital* [1968, 2nd edn], trans. Ben Brewster. London: New Left Books.
Balibar, Renée (1974) *Les Français fictifs: le rapport des styles littéraires au français national*. Paris: Hachette.
*Balibar, Renée (1978) 'An Example of Literary Work in France: George Sand's "La mare au diable"/"The Devil's Pool" of 1846', trans. John Coombes. In *1848: The Sociology of Literature*, ed. Francis Barker, John Coombes, Peter Hulme, Colin Mercer and David Musselwhite, Colchester: University of Essex.
Barthes, Roland (1977) *Image-Music-Text*, trans. Stephen Heath. London: Fontana. Contains:
[1971] 'Writers, Intellectuals, Teachers'.
Belsey, Catherine (1980) *Critical Practice*. London: Methuen.
Burke, Edmund (1793) *Reflections on the Revolution in France*, 12th edn, [1790]. London: J. Dodsley.
Centre for Contemporary Cultural Studies (1981) *Unpopular Education: Schooling and Social Democracy in England since 1944*. London: Hutchinson.
Davies, Tony (1981) 'Education, Ideology and Literature' [1978]. In *Culture, Ideology and Social Process*, ed. Tony Bennett, Graham Martin, Colin Mercer and Janet Woollacott, London: Batsford.
Deleuze, Gilles (1977) 'Intellectuals and Power: A Conversation between Michel Foucault and Gilles Deleuze' [1972]. In Michel Foucault, *Language, Counter-Memory, Practice*, trans. Donald Bouchard and Sherry Simon, Oxford: Blackwell.
Deleuze, Gilles and Guattari, Félix (1981) *Rhizome* [1976], trans. Paul Foss and Paul Patton. *I&C*, 8, 49–71.
Doyle, Brian (1982) 'The hidden history of English studies'. In *Re- Reading English*, ed. Peter Widdowson, London: Methuen.
Eagleton, Terry (1983) *Literary Theory: An Introduction*. Oxford: Blackwell.
Eagleton, Terry (1984) *The Function of Criticism: From* The Spectator *to*

Post-Structuralism. London: Verso and New Left Books.

Easthope, Antony (1983) 'The Trajectory of *Screen*, 1971–79'. In *The Politics of Theory*, ed. Francis Barker, Peter Hulme, Margaret Iversen and Diana Loxley, Colchester: University of Essex.

Edelman, Bernard (1979) *Ownership of the Image: Elements for a Marxist Theory of Law* [1973], trans. Elizabeth Kingdom. London: Routledge and Kegan Paul.

Finn, Dan and Grant, Neil and Johnson, Richard (1978) 'Social Democracy, Education and the Crisis'. In *On Ideology*. Centre for Contemporary Cultural Studies, London: Hutchinson.

*Foucault, Michel (1967) *Madness and Civilization: A History of Insanity in the Age of Reason* [1961], trans. Richard Howard. London: Tavistock.

Foucault, Michel (1969) *L'archéologie du savoir*. Paris: Gallimard.

Foucault, Michel (1970) *The Order of Things: An Archaeology of the Human Sciences* [1966]. London: Tavistock.

*Foucault, Michel (1972) *The Archaeology of Knowledge* [1969], trans. A. M. Sheridan Smith. London: Tavistock.

Foucault, Michel (1973) *The Birth of the Clinic: An Archaeology of Medical Perception* [1963], trans. A. M. Sheridan. London: Tavistock.

*Foucault, Michel (1977a) *Language, Counter-Memory, Practice*, trans. Donald Bouchard and Sherry Simon. Oxford: Blackwell. Contains:

[1969] 'What Is an Author?'

[1971a] 'History of Systems of Thought'.

[1971b] 'Revolutionary Action: "Until Now"'.

[1972] 'Intellectuals and Power: A Conversation between Michel Foucault and Gilles Deleuze'.

*Foucault, Michel (1977b) *Discipline and Punish: The Birth of the Prison* [1975], trans. Alan Sheridan. Harmondsworth: Allen Lane, Penguin Books.

Foucault, Michel (ed.) (1978) *I, Pierre Rivière, having slaughtered my mother, my sister and my brother* . . . . [1973]. Harmondsworth: Penguin Books.

*Foucault, Michel (1979) *The History of Sexuality, Volume 1: An Introduction* [1976], trans. Robert Hurley. Harmondsworth: Allen Lane, Penguin Books.

*Foucault, Michel (1980a) *Power/Knowledge: Selected Interviews and other Writings 1972–1977*, trans. Colin Gordon. Brighton: Harvester. Contains:

[1972] 'On Popular Justice: A Discussion with Maoists'.

[1975a] 'Prison Talk'.

[1975b] 'Body/Power'.

[1976] 'Questions on Geography'.

[1977a] 'Two Lectures'.

[1977b] 'Truth and Power'.

[1977c] 'Power and Strategies'.

[1977d] 'The Eye of Power'.

[1977e] 'The Confession of the Flesh'.

Foucault, Michel (1980b) 'The History of Sexuality: Interview' [1977], trans. Geoff Bennington. *Oxford Literary Review*, 4, 2, 3–14.

*Foucault, Michel (1981) 'The Order of Discourse' [1971], trans. Ian McLeod. In *Untying the Text: A Post-Structuralist Reader*, ed. Robert Young, London: Routledge and Kegan Paul.

Foucault, Michel (1982) 'Afterword: The Subject and Power'. In Hubert L. Dreyfus and Paul Rabinow, *Michel Foucault: Beyond Structuralism and Hermeneutics*, Brighton: Harvester.

Foucault, Michel (1984a) *Histoire de la sexualité: 2. L'usage des plaisirs.* Paris: Gallimard.

Foucault, Michel (1984b) *Histoire de la sexualité: 3. Le souci de soi.* Paris: Gallimard.

Giddens, Anthony (1982) 'A Reply to my Critics'. *Theory, Culture and Society*, 1, 2, 107–13.

Gordon, Colin (1979) 'Other Inquisitions'. *I&C*, 6, 23–46.

Gramsci, Antonio (1979) *Letters from Prison* [1946], trans. Lynne Lawner. London: Quartet Books.

*Hall, Stuart (1978) 'Some Problems with the Ideology/Subject Couplet'. *Ideology and Consciousness*, 3, 113–21.

Harvey, Sylvia (1978) *May '68 and Film Culture.* London: British Film Institute.

Hawkes, Terence (1977) *Structuralism and Semiotics.* London: Methuen.

Hindess, Barry (1977) *Philosophy and Methodology in the Social Sciences.* Hassocks: Harvester.

Hindess, Barry and Hirst, Paul (1975) *Pre-Capitalist Modes of Production.* London: Routledge and Kegan Paul.

*Hindess, Barry and Hirst, Paul (1977a) *Mode of Production and Social Formation.* London: Macmillan.

Hindess, Barry and Hirst, Paul and Cutler, Antony and Hussain, Athar (1977b) *Marx's 'Capital' and Capitalism Today*, vol. 1. London: Routledge and Kegan Paul.

Hindess, Barry and Hirst, Paul and Cutler, Antony and Hussain, Athar (1978) *Marx's 'Capital' and Capitalism Today*, vol. 2. London: Routledge and Kegan Paul.

*Hirst, Paul (1979) *On Law and Ideology.* London: Macmillan. Contains two earlier publications:

[1976a] 'Problems and Advances in the Theory of Ideology'.

[1976b] 'Althusser and the Theory of Ideology'.

Johnson, Richard (1972) *The French Communist Party versus the Students: Revolutionary Politics in May-June 1968*. New Haven and London: Yale University Press.

Laclau, Ernesto (1980) 'Populist Rupture and Discourse', trans. Jim Grealy. *Screen Education*, 34, 87–93.

*Lecourt, Dominique (1975) *Marxism and Epistemology: Bachelard, Canguilhem and Foucault*, trans. Ben Brewster. London: New Left Books. Contains:
[1972] 'On Archaeology and Knowledge (Michel Foucault)'.

Macherey, Pierre (1977) 'Problems of Reflection', trans. John Coombes. In *Literature, Society and the Sociology of Literature*, ed. Francis Barker, John Coombes, Peter Hulme, David Musselwhite and Richard Osborne, Colchester: University of Essex.

Marx, Karl (1976) *Capital*, vol. 1 [1867], trans. Ben Fowkes. Harmondsworth: Penguin Books.

Miller, Peter (1980) 'The Territory of the Psychiatrist'. *I&C*, 7, 63–105.

*Moi, Toril (1983) 'Sexual/Textual Politics'. In *The Politics of Theory*, ed. Francis Barker, Peter Hulme, Margaret Iversen and Diana Loxley, Colchester: University of Essex.

Paine, Thomas (1791) *Rights of Man: Being an Answer to Mr. Burke's attack on the French Revolution*, part 1. London: J. Johnson.

*Pêcheux, Michel (1978) 'Are the Masses an Inanimate Object?' In *Linguistic Variation: Models and Methods*, ed. David Sankoff, New York: Academic Press.

*Pêcheux, Michel (1982) *Language, Semantics and Ideology: Stating the Obvious* [1975], trans. Harbans Nagpal. London: Macmillan. Contains new appendix:
[1982] 'The French Political Winter: Beginning of a Rectification (Postscript for English Readers)'.

Pêcheux, Michel (1983) 'Ideology: Fortress or Paradoxical Space'. In *Rethinking Ideology: A Marxist Debate*, ed. Sakari Hänninen and Leena Paldán, New York: International General.

*Poulantzas, Nicos (1978) *State, Power, Socialism* [1978], trans. Patrick Camiller. London: New Left Books.

Price, Richard (1790) *A Discourse on the Love of our Country*, 6th edn. London: T. Cadell.

Saussure, Ferdinand de (1974) *Course in General Linguistics* [1916], trans. Wade Baskin. London: Fontana.

Seale, Patrick and McConville, Maureen (1968) *French Revolution 1968*. London: Heinemann, and Harmondsworth: Penguin Books.

Singer, Daniel (1970) *Prelude to Revolution: France in May 1968*. London: Jonathan Cape.

Skillen, Tony (1978) 'Post-Marxist Modes of Production'. *Radical*

138   *Bibliography*

Philosophy, 20, 3–8.

Soboul, Albert (1974) *The French Revolution 1787–1799* [1962], 2 vols, trans. Alan Forrest and Colin Jones. London: New Left Books.

Thompson, John O. (1981) 'Real Pictures, Real Pleasures?' *Screen Education*, 38, 89–94.

*Vološinov, V. N. (1973) *Marxism and the Philosophy of Language* [1930], trans. L. Matejka and I. R. Titunik. New York: Seminar Press.

Williams, Raymond (1977) *Marxism and Literature*. Oxford: Oxford University Press.

Notes on further reading

While the foregoing list of references provides a starting-place, there are some additional items I would like to mention. In Althusser's work, I have concentrated on issues of ideology and discourse leaving aside his early essays. These, different and still important, are collected mainly in *For Marx* [1965] trans. Ben Brewster (London: New Left Books, 1977) and in *Montesquieu, Rousseau, Marx: Politics and History*, trans. Ben Brewster (London: New Left Books, 1972). Of interest alongside the post-1968 essays I have discussed are two pieces on 'The Historic Significance of the 22nd Congress' [1976] and on 'The Crisis of Marxism' [1977]. The first, focused on the PCF, is contained in the book by E. Balibar, trans. Grahame Lock, cited below; a slightly different version, trans. Ben Brewster, may be found in *New Left Review* 104 (1977), 3–22. The second, trans. Grahame Lock, is in *Marxism Today*, 22 (1978), 215–20, 227.

There are helpful discussions of Althusser's theories in the volume *On Ideology* (London: Hutchinson, 1978) produced by the Centre for Contemporary Cultural Studies. In addition, several journals have taken up the arguments: notably, *New Left Review*; also, if selectively, *Screen*; and, at best ambiguously, *Economy and Society*. But some responses, averse to the Leninist standpoint of Althusser's work, have been simply dismissive, for example, E. P. Thompson, *The Poverty of Theory, and Other Essays* (London: Merlin, 1978). In France, Althusser's theories have occasioned much debate and positive consideration.

Besides Pêcheux's key developments for the theory of discourse and the researches of Renée Balibar (see references), important related work in the fields of philosophy and the history of the sciences has been carried out by Étienne Balibar and Dominique Lecourt. Two interesting articles by Étienne Balibar are 'On Literature as an Ideological Form' [1978], and 'Marx, the joker in the pack' [1981]. The former, written jointly with Pierre Macherey, is contained in Robert Young, ed., *Untying the Text: A Post-Structuralist Reader* (London: Routledge and Kegan Paul, 1981); and the latter, trans. David Watson, appears in *Economy and Society*, 14 (1985), 1–27. Balibar's important book *On the Dictatorship of the Proletariat* [1976] is available in English, trans. Grahame Lock (London: New Left Books, 1977), as are Dominique Lecourt's studies of *Marxism and Epistemology* (see references) and *Proletarian Science? The Case of Lysenko* [1976], trans. Ben Brewster (London: New Left Books, 1977).

The development of theory and analysis of discourse at the Centre National de la Recherche Scientifique (Paris), in particular by Michel Pêcheux, and also by Paul Henry (see *Le mauvais outil: langue, sujet et discours*, Paris: Klincksieck, 1977), and others, is beginning to receive some notice outside France: Pêcheux's work is discussed by Mark Cousins, 'Jokes and their relation to the mode of production', *Economy and Society*, 14 (1985), 94–112; by Colin MacCabe, 'On discourse', *Economy and Society*, 8 (1979), 279–307; and by Roger Woods, 'Discourse analysis: the work of Michel Pêcheux', *Ideology and Consciousness*, 2 (1977), 57–79. *La langue introuvable* (Paris: Maspero, 1981) written jointly by Françoise Gadet and Michel Pêcheux, also calls for attention.

The arguments put forward by Hindess and Hirst have had most impact in the social sciences, and they have been given a ready forum by the journal *Economy and Society*. *Radical Philosophy* has run helpful critiques, and further critical discussion is given in John Mepham and David-Hillel Rubin, eds, *Issues in Marxist Philosophy, Volume III: Epistemology, Science, Ideology* (Brighton: Harvester, 1979).

Two journals, the *Oxford Literary Review* and *Ideology and Consciousness* (later retitled *I&C*), have been especially useful in incorporating many of the uncollected essays and interviews of Michel Foucault. The latter has also included studies deploying Foucault's archaeological methods, such as Karen Jones and Kevin Williamson, 'The Birth of the Schoolroom', *I&C*, 6 (1979), 58–110, as well as translations of sometimes related essays, such as Deleuze and Guattari, *Rhizome* (see references). Foucault's various writings are attracting increasing attention and there are a number of commentaries which, while playing down the materialism of Foucault's studies, are helpful: notably, Alan Sheridan, *Michel Foucault: The Will to Truth* (London: Tavistock, 1980) and Hubert L. Dreyfus and Paul Rabinow, *Michel Foucault: Beyond Structuralism and Hermeneutics* (Brighton: Harvester, 1982).

Index